O'Hara Is For

cigarettes, Goldwater, Charles de Gaulle, firearms.

He's Against

Robert Kennedy, Audrey Hepburn, writers who turn down Nobel Prizes and White House dinner invitations, Birchites.

And He's Just Not Sure About Abraham Lincoln.

Here they are—the salty, slashing, deliberately infuriating, wickedly humorous columns that made the nation's editors drop O'Hara like a hot potato. You may delight in what John O'Hara has to say . . . or you may disagree violently. But one thing's for sure, he explodes a heated reaction every time.

"Marvelously, intelligently, merrily malicious"
—Jack O'Brian, N.Y. JOURNAL AMERICAN

"O'Hara the journalist can be every bit as controversial as O'Hara the novelist." —CHICAGO TRIBUNE

JOHN O'HARA was born in Pottsville, Pennsylvania, in 1905. His first novel, Appointment in Samarra, was published in 1934. He successfully ventured onto Broadway to write the book for the adaptation of his story Pal Joey (later the winner of the New York Critics Circle and Donaldson awards for the best musical of 1952). His literary production has continued unabated over the years; his bestselling novels include Butterfield 8, A Rage to Live, the 1955 National Book Award winner Ten North Frederick, From the Terrace and The Lockwood Concern (published in a Signet edition).

My Turn

JOHN O'HARA

A SIGNET BOOK

Published by The New American Library

SIGNET TRADEMARK REG. U.S. PAT. OFF. AND FOREIGN COUNTRIES
REGISTERED TRADEMARK—MARCA REGISTRADA
HECHO EN CHICAGO, U.S.A.

SIGNET BOOKS are published by
The New American Library, Inc.,
1301 Avenue of the Americas, New York, New York 10019

PRINTED IN THE UNITED STATES OF AMERICA

To

JIM FORRESTAL

Foreword

And even if nobody reads me, have I wasted my time in entertaining myself so many idle hours with such useful and agreeable thoughts? In modeling this figure upon myself, I have been so often obliged to shape and compose myself in order to bring myself out that the model has thereby become firm and has to some extent formed itself. Painting myself for others, I have painted my inner self in clearer colors than were my first ones. I have no more made my book than my book has made me: a book consubstantial with its author, concerned only with me, a vital part of my life; not having an outside and alien concern and objective like all other books. Have I wasted my time by taking account of myself so continually, so carefully? For they who survey themselves only in their minds, and occasionally aloud, do not examine themselves so fundamentally nor penetrate so deeply as does he who makes it his study, his work, and his trade, who with all his faith, with all his strength, binds himself to make a lasting account . . .

I have not bothered to italicize the preceding words or to put them between quotation marks because all my learned friends will immediately recognize them as the work of Michel de Montaigne. One or two, perhaps the anonymous reviewer for *Time* and the semi-anonymous Granville Hicks, may not be able to say offhand which of the *Essays* the quotation came from. But the *Time* person will pass that buck to a researcher; and Granville Hicks, who surely has nothing better to do, will have a good excuse to steep himself in that intellectual atmosphere that is too rarefied for anyone but him. (It would be funny as hell if he should come upon J. Donald Adams gasping for breath.)

The aptness of the Montaigne quotation is not complete. I take my Montaigne in small doses, and as Montaigne admitted in another essay, we sometimes find ourselves rereading something as though we had never seen it before. I rather hope that that will be the experience for some of the readers of this volume. The pieces were, of course, written for newspaper syndication, and will have been seen by several million men and women who will not buy this book and by conjectural thousands who do. When I stopped writing the column "My Turn" I got about a thousand letters from readers who —with a single exception—said they were sorry to see me quit. This book is intended for them and for those like them who did not write.

I probably did not change anyone's mind about anything. During the active existence of the column I got several letters from people who professed to be admirers of my fictional writing, but who were so outraged or disappointed in one or more of these pieces that they swore to God they'd never read me again. To that I say, "Nuts." The small bully, the potential or actual book-burner, was nearly always an ironbound, conformist liberal, who makes a lot of noise in behalf of free speech and against censorship. But it cannot be said too often that intimidation of one sort is as evil as intimidation of another, and the man or woman who threatens you with one kind of extinction is threatening you with another. In my view, by the way, a bribe is no prettier than a threat. The people who tell you to go easy, or to lay off a little, are only a couple of sentences away from, "Or else!"

This is certainly the most appropriate place to tell what happened to my column. Harry Guggenheim, a nice man who owns the newspaper *Newsday* and its syndicate, never interfered with anything I wrote. Contractually, he could not, but except for some kidding about my conservatism, he did not attempt to influence me. My guarantee was for $1000 a week, minimum, which was paid me by the syndicate. The column was published in *Newsday* and about forty-five other papers, big and little. When the other papers began to drop the column, it became an expensive feature for *Newsday*. In theory, *Newsday* was absorbing a larger proportion of my guarantee.

Guggenheim then suggested a change in what he called the "format" of the column. He wanted me to stop commenting on current events and substitute a short story every week. That, of course, I would not do, and I am convinced that Guggenheim believed he was giving me an out. Even Guggenheim could not afford to pay me the kind of money I would demand for a weekly short story. So, in accordance with the terms of our contract, I duly notified him that after such-and-such a date, the column "My Turn" would cease to exist. Polite and friendly letters were exchanged, and to no one's great surprise, John Steinbeck was hired to write a column. Steinbeck's column is called "Letters to Alicia," Alicia being the late wife of Guggenheim and the daughter of Joseph Medill Patterson, founder of the New York *Daily News*. Mrs. Guggenheim, who did not see eye-to-eye with her father after he fell out with Franklin D. Roosevelt, was the founder of *Newsday*. She would be much more likely to get, and read, letters from John Steinbeck than from me, and I am sure she has stopped spinning in her grave now that I am no longer in her paper.

But I'll turn up on a newspaper somewhere. I always do.

J. O'H.

December 1965
Princeton, New Jersey

October 3, 1964

Let's get off to a really bad start.

I have signed a contract to write a weekly message, of which this is the first. At the end of a year either party to the contract can terminate it, with a certain amount of hard feelings on both sides. I would like all you fun people to enjoy yourselves or to have apoplexy as you read what I have to say. But let it be clearly understood that I took this job because I was persuaded that I could do it without neglecting my work as novelist and author of short stories, and because I would be getting paid for sounding off on more or less topical subjects. The pay here is good, but it will all go to one of my least favorite charities, the federal government. My travel expenses are guaranteed, but as I never go anywhere without my wife, and her expenses are not deductible, I do not expect to be able to chisel much there.

In a way I am sitting pretty, as independent as a wealthy amateur, but an amateur I am not. (Wealthy I am not, either, but it is true that I could get by for the rest of my life without working.) I am strictly a professional, have been one for forty years and will be one as long as I live. I love to work, which is a lucky thing for me since I have always had to work. I do not mean to sound virtuous about work. If it were a kind of work that I did not enjoy—and I have done plenty of that—I would not love work for work's sake. As it has turned out, however, I have been able to make a good living at the kind of work I take pleasure in and derive satisfaction from and end sentences with.

And it has been and is work, make no mistake about that. It has often been a tough fight, Mom. Consequently I withdrew from the popularity contest a long while ago. I have a journalistic acquaintance who has always shown a nice flair, a better than average deftness with the language, but he writes as though he were afraid to offend his next dinner-party hostess. His job requires him to express personal opinions, but with those imaginary hostesses looking over his shoulder as he writes, he is overcome with caution. Timidity of opinion will get you nowhere, and writing for anyone's approval but your own will get you there fast. So I shall make no effort to present my opinions in equivocal style. You will always know which side I am on.

Indeed, I fully expect that there will be readers who will so seldom agree with me that I may lose them in a few weeks. I expect to lose some right now, before they have given themselves a chance to come under my spell. That will be their loss, more than mine, since I will be doing business at this stand for at least a year. My books have sold many millions in many languages, and there is no new compliment or abuse that is likely to be turning up in my mail. I have had experience with the bullies who operate as individuals or in pressure groups. Only once did I lose a job as a result of pressure. A man who worked for Hearst told a cowardly publisher that I was a Communist, and the publisher found a way to get rid of me. It was years later that I found out why. This is not to be taken as a friendly nod in the direction of Communists or people who play along with them. I was a lifelong, straight-ticket Democrat until Adlai Stevenson popped up, and I have been a straight-line Republican ever since. But I know how far people who do not agree with you will go to get you fired.

My original intention for this first appearance was to compile a list of my likes and dislikes. It would be an easy column to write, and it might save some readers the trouble of reading my second column. However, I decided against that. I am not really going to try to convert anyone to my way of thinking. There will be enough of that this fall, and as a political buff I probably will expose myself to more of it and get more tired of it than my readers. What I intend to offer in these messages are comments on the human race in my time, as seen by my prejudiced eye. Entertainment, rather than instruction, should result, although I probably will toss in some bits of information of the sort that clutter up my mind. The whole thing may turn out to be a bomb, but if it does, what of it? When I was a young reporter I scarcely ever let a day go by without reading Heywood Broun and FPA, and I thought I would never get used to doing without them. But I have. One does. Therefore I have no illusions about my own indispensability. I have, of course, few doubts about my wisdom. In this wondrous world you can say almost anything that comes into your mind, and sooner or later you may turn out to have been right.

Who would have thought, for instance, that the king of England would give up his throne for a simple American aristocrat? Who would have dared predict that the New York Giants would be playing by candlelight?

October 10, 1964

When I first lit and inhaled a cigarette I knew I was not taking a Horlick's malted milk tablet. Although I was only twelve years old, or maybe thirteen, I knew that smoking was not good for me. Nevertheless I boldly put a match to my Condax (or maybe it was a Melachrino Number 9), somewhat less boldly pulled the smoke into my lungs, and I've been at it ever since. For fifty years I've been at it. Before I started to inhale Turkish cigarettes I had learned to blow smoke through my nostrils, the smoke of Cubebs, of corn silk, of Sweet Caporals. But it was sissy stuff to fake inhaling by letting the smoke trickle out your nose, and to the Irish lads at St. Patrick's School I was already enough of a sissy because I lived where I lived and attended dancing class. They called me lace-curtain and said I was a dirty ristycrat (the aristocrats said I was Irish, which was invective enough), but when I became a cigarette fiend and had to be careful about getting the nicotine stains off my fingers, my schoolmates realized that I was wicked, and wicked and sissy did not go together. I became such a confirmed addict of butts that for economic reasons I had to switch from those straw-tipped ones in cardboard boxes to the plain ones in paper packs. Luckies, Omars, and, when I was flush, Fatimas. As an altar boy I smoked in the sacristy, as a budding junior delinquent I smoked at the movies, in front of the drugstore, on trolley cars and trains and everywhere else but home, where only guests were invited to light up.

But I never thought I was taking a malted milk tablet. I smoked in the beginning because it was forbidden, and I kept smoking because I liked it. Obviously it had not stunted my growth; I was six feet tall when I was fifteen years old, and I could and did ride a horse thirty-five miles in a day. In prep school they measured my lung capacity and it was second to that of the captain of the track team, who was also taller and heavier than I. (And who, incidentally, smoked as much as I did.)

These reminiscences are my answer to the medical zealots who are getting very close to the fanaticism which will mean that a drag on a cigarette will be punishable by law. You think not? Well, the government health people are extremely angry because cigarette sales, which had fallen off, are on the increase again. There is lobbying for a bill that will require the manufacturers to label each pack in such a way as to warn the smoker that he is committing suicide with every puff. In New York City a woman health-department doctor has announced that clinics are to be opened to help those miserable citizens who can't give up the weed. Big Brother and Big Sister are at it again. The pious mutterings of the cigarette companies, their advertising agencies, and the broadcasting people are the usual gutless performances of such people when they are threatened by the threat of government interference. Cigarette advertising has always been pretty disgusting, whether it was the pseudo-patriotism of "Lucky Strike Green Has Gone to War" or the Madison Avenue grammarians' "Winston tastes good like a cigarette should." Now the ad boys and the tobacco companies are promising to be good boys and do as little as possible to encourage kids to start using gaspers. I am in my sixtieth year, and as of my last checkup I didn't get lung cancer, in spite of the smoking I have done. Therefore I am living proof (as is another author, W. Somerset Maugham, now in his ninetieth year) that the cigarette habit is not fatal. If the Big Brothers and Sisters of government and medicine were right, Maugham and I ought to be dead by this time. Lung cancer may get me in the end, as something will get Somerset Maugham, but the argument that the Big Brethren are presenting, that cigarette-smoking will of itself kill you, is just not so. Nevertheless the argument will continue, legislation will be enacted, and a brand-new enforcement agency will be set up by Big Bro.

Do you know anyone who regards cigarette-smoking as a health measure? Does anyone know anyone who regards cigarette-smoking as a health measure? On the other hand does anyone know anyone who just can't wait to start reading a Big Brother tract after that first cup of coffee in the morning? (Notice I didn't say light up one of Big Brother's tracts.) I stopped drinking alcoholic beverages eleven years ago and have not had a drink since then. If I had gone on drinking I'd have died of causes directly related to booze. But in my eleven years on the wagon no one has ever said, "Please don't have another cigarette, John. Remember, you're driving." And yet the same hysteria that afflicted the Prohibitionists is now evident among the anti-cigarettists. Now they use fear, contributing their nasty little bit of climate of fear that they somehow managed to attribute to both Senator McCarthy (the Joe one) and the hydrogen bomb. In the old days the Prohibitionists showed pictures of Pop lapping it up and blowing the week's pay in the corner saloon, but that won't work now against cigarettes. Fear is the gimmick today. We're not just chicken. Big Brother is turning the nation into a grand and glorious poultry farm.

October 17, 1964

Whenever I tend to have a doubt about voting Republican this year, as when Senator Goldwater says something I don't like, I think of the alternatives.

I think of the reluctant man who four years ago gave in to Bobby Kennedy in Los Angeles and who is now President of the United States.

I think of Bobby Kennedy.

I think of Pierre Salinger.

And I think of Hubert Humphrey.

I cannot take Senator Salinger very seriously. He seems an amiable, fast-talking little man, with a bad case of Potomac fever, cigar ashes spilling down his front, and nothing terribly sinister about him. He happens to be running against an old friend of mine, George Murphy, and I hope Murphy beats him, not only because Murphy is my friend but because Salinger symbolizes the cynical arrogance that has characterized the entire Kennedy operation. The ugliness at Dallas a year ago did not change that. I shed a tear for John F. Kennedy, not from any fondness for the man but because he was the victim of a stupid, brutal act in the prime of his life. As never before, I fully understood how a defeated southerner could weep when Lincoln was murdered. Ugliness, brutality, stupidity, against which there is no defense, no protection. But the horrible irony is that both Booth and Oswald were afflicted with some of the same wiseguy attitude that has been the curse of the Kennedy boys, and I suspect was no small item in the character of Lincoln. The ugliness at Dallas did not change what had gone on before, and it apparently has not changed the Kennedy perspective. Consequently we have Salinger in California and Bobby Kennedy in New York, the Louis Vuitton carpetbaggers.

As a Republican who was a straight-ticket Democrat until Adlai Stevenson began running, I give high priority to the defeat of Salinger and Bobby Kennedy. I cannot get quite so steamed up over Mr. Johnson, who was arm-twisted into the vice-presidency (a dose of his own medicine, you might say, in view of the politicking he had done so effectively in the Senate). He is an uninspiring, uninspired man, whom no one loathes and no one loves. He is a mixture of weariness and wariness, and in the argot of the Navy, a mustang who never wanted his flag. Circumstances have put him on the spot.

It is, of course, the spot that every professional politician sees himself in at one time or another. If you pitch four innings for Gibbsville High School, you cannot fail to mittyize yourself as the hero of the World Series, and it is a dream to live on because the chances are so great against its ever coming true. But Mr. Johnson mittyized, and his dream came true, and there's absolutely no turning back. He just has to stick it out. One of the first things he did on his own was to shake free of those Instant Adamses, the Kennedys; but he cannot shake free of the Democratic Party oligarchy and hope to win. He has to be Big Labor's boy; he has to go along with the foreign policy that was created by Harry Hopkins and God knows who else. The Liberal Establishment requires undeviating conformity, and as a consequence Mr. Johnson may end up a balletomane. Already he has been made captive by the intellectuals, who are trying hard to invest him with qualities and tastes that suit them but not him. They want him to be Adlai Stevenson, and he just ain't, but he let his arm be twisted four years ago.

I think it's time the Lawrence Welk people had their say. The Lester Lanin and Dizzy Gillespie people have been on too long. When the country is in trouble, like war kind of trouble, man, it is the Lawrence Welk people who can be depended upon, all the way. Those men and women who voted for Nixon have not vanished from the earth. Most of them are still around, and most of them will vote for Goldwater. I am going to vote for Goldwater because he is one of those people, and because he has not had to make the commitments that Mr. Johnson has had to make. I am an admirer of General Charles de Gaulle and of Sir Alec Douglas-Home, two men who never caught the fancy of the people who have been so violently opposed to Goldwater. De Gaulle is a nationalist, as Douglas-Home is a nationalist, as Goldwater is a nationalist, as Khrushchev is an internationalist. The Lawrence Welk people of France and Britain put de Gaulle and Douglas-Home in office. In the Soviet Union there are no Lawrence Welk people, but of course there are a great many balletomanes. In this country the balletomane vote is solidly anti-Goldwater, and I can think of worse reasons for supporting him. If I had to limit myself to only one reason for supporting Goldwater, that reason might be Hubert Humphrey. Now there's a man to give you a chill when you consider where his mittyizing might put him.

October 24, 1964

The gradual but steady approach of the moviemakers toward their ultimate goal is much more interesting to watch than the movies themselves. In, I should say, about five years it will be possible to go to your neighborhood picture palace or the local drive-in and there see the kind of movie that in times past was available only at stag smokers. It will all be there; explicit, uncut, wide screen, in color, and dreary. And those who don't happen to catch it in a theater will be able to see it a year later at home on TV. This may turn out to be a partial solution to the population explosion. The movie producers will have made sex so unattractively commonplace that nothing will stimulate the cosmic urge, as we used to call it, and the birth rate will drop accordingly except in a few isolated localities where there are no movie theaters and TV reception is bad.

At various stages of my life I have been a professional movie reviewer, a line of endeavor which, until radio and TV came along, was the lowest form of critical activity. At present, movie reviewing is to TV reviewing what theater reviewing once was to movie reviewing. When I could not go to the movies on a pass, I paid. I was a movie fan who saw *Tillie's Punctured Romance* when it was brand-new, and continued my devotion through *The Perils of Pauline*, the D. W. Griffith epics, and on into the talkies. I even got sufficiently highbrow to learn some of the technical stuff about picture-making. And Louella Parsons herself is on record as having said that I made a "fortune" out of the film industry. Well, that's true. I did make it, and was temporary custodian of it for the federal government.

But I hardly ever go to the movies any more. The last movie I saw was *Night of the Iguana,* and before that I had last seen *La Dolce Vita.* There was a gap between them of at least two years, and that two-year hiatus was just long enough to show the progress the moviemakers were making toward their ultimate goal. The Italian film (which I consider a work of the cinematic art) did not disturb me one bit. I can't recall a single sequence that was meant to shock the audience for the sake of shock. But the American film seemed to have been put together after a series of conferences in which the director and the screenwriter had uppermost in mind their hope of giving the audience a jolt. When the Tennessee Williams playscript (not one of his best) did not suit their purpose, they contrived some little shocker of their own, like having the ex-clergyman and the nymphet walk barefoot on broken glass. Never, by the way, have cut and bleeding feet healed so quickly and painlessly, and without stitches. The language is tiresomely profane or, in other spots, intramurally special to the world of the homosexual. There are splendid, nearly faultless performances by Richard Burton, Deborah Kerr, and Ava Gardner, for which the director need not take any credit, since a director could have controlled Miss Gardner's stridency. (I don't think the director, John Huston, is going to insist at this late date that he showed Mr. Burton and Miss Kerr how to act.) But after the naughty language and the scenes such as Miss Gardner's with the beach boys, what do you do for an encore? Where do you go next? The obvious, inevitable answer is "Bed," and no subtleties about it. No Rouben Mamoulian crashing of cymbals, no Lubitsch touches, no panning to the moon rising high or the turbulent surf, the oldtime symbolism that was once so difficult to get past the Hays Office. It's got to be for real.

Very well. We're about ready for it. If I were more profound or more painstakingly thorough, I could reason out a theory that Joe Levine is not merely a movie producer but a symbol of our resistance to the machine. I am less and less convinced of the durability of the race of man, and if we are about to crowd ourselves out of existence, or to be transistorized into atrophy, the sky is no longer the limit. Nothing is. That being the case, Hollywood ought to invite Ingmar Bergman to come over and take complete charge of motion picture production, and the film division of the Library of Congress ought to spread the word that it is looking for positives and negatives of those 16-mm. movies that have instructed and delighted two generations of redblooded sports. These prints should be shown to Bergman so that he does not repeat them when he takes over the industry. After all, we don't want Grandpa walking out of a 1970 movie saying, "Hell, I saw this the night I was initiated into the Friendly Order of Cattle Rustlers."

I have to confess that *Rebecca of Sunnybrook Farm* bored me.

October 31, 1964

Several Norwegian newspapers have expressed misgivings about the award of the Nobel peace prize to Dr. Martin Luther King. Their feeling is that Dr. King's career has been national rather than world-wide, and that he therefore does not qualify under the rules. Since the Norwegians have cast some doubt on Dr. King's eligibility, I am emboldened to make a few comments of my own. I don't think he should have got it, either, and naturally I am going to tell you why.

For the most part I have been sympathetic to Dr. King, as I believe are most people in the United States. His proclaimed policy of nonviolence is praiseworthy, and there is no possible way to estimate the number of lives it may have saved. But Dr. King got off an airplane in New York during the Gilligan affair excitement and declared to the TV audience that "murder" had been committed. (Gilligan is a police lieutenant who shot and killed a young man who attacked him with a knife, and the grand jury refused to indict him.) Just in case the TV audience missed it the first time, Dr. King repeated the word murder. The first time might have been a slip of the tongue; the second time was deliberate.

In the newspaper business we are awfully careful about how we use that word, murder. One chain of papers barred the word in any circumstances, just as another paper on which I once worked had a rule against the use of the word blood except in medical stories. It therefore surprised me that the TV people allowed Dr. King to utter the word twice in the same interview. Lt. Gilligan had not yet been indicted

23

on any charge, and as I said before, the grand jury subsequently failed to indict him when his case came up. Gilligan, incidentally, is a cop who had been decorated nineteen times during his career as a police officer. Nevertheless Dr. King, who had not even been in New York at the time of the shooting, characterized the policeman's act as "murder" and did so at a time when all hell was ready to break loose. If that's nonviolence, what is meant by rabble-rousing? Dr. King is no Malcolm X or Cassius Clay; he had been regarded as the man who more than anyone else in the United States had the trust of both Negroes and whites. He had had plenty of time to think of what he was going to say to the interviewers at the airport. He is an articulate man, who generally speaks in paragraphs rather than sentences. He is a clergyman, accustomed to addressing his congregations from the pulpit. But his repeated use of the word murder was reckless and irresponsible, and I wonder what he thinks of it now that he has been given the Nobel peace prize. Apart from the fact that a grand jury, having considered all the facts in the case, refused to indict the police officer, and thereby in effect established his innocence of the charge, there remains the negative fact that Dr. King has never to my knowledge withdrawn his accusation.

This was a New York County grand jury, and not a panel of rednecks and hardboots and woolhats, whose findings might have been suspect. The task of a grand jury is not to determine a defendant's guilt or innocence; its task is to decide whether the facts in a case warrant a court trial. But if the grand jury does not return a true bill, that ends it, so far as the judicial process is concerned. In this case, however, an outstanding Negro leader had twice characterized the shooting as murder, and when the grand jury failed to indict Gilligan for murder, manslaughter, or anything else, it was Dr. King's duty to make some amends for his terribly serious charge. Dr. King knows the law; more important than that, he knows something about justice.

Martin Luther King is thirty-five years old, and he has come a long way. He is, I believe, the youngest man ever to be awarded the Nobel peace prize, and he may not have been quite ready for it. But the award is a fait accompli; it is on the books and as long as there is a World Almanac, or a world, Dr. King's name will be recorded in the history of 1964. He has announced that the money—about $50,000—will be put to good use, and I haven't the slightest doubt about that. The question in my mind is not whether he qualified under the terms of the sphere of his influence, which disturbed the Norwegian newspapers. He has that influence now, by virtue of the prestige that attaches to the winner of the prize. He now has six names: Martin Luther King Nobel Prize Winner. That will be his name for the rest of his life, and his children and grandchildren will partake of the benefits of his prestige. But if he has come a long way from Detroit, he likewise has a long way to go. He can certainly count on at least twenty-five active years ahead, and I am not going to be around to see how he comes out. I believe that the award was both timely and premature. If I turn out to be wrong, the whole country will benefit by Dr. King's proof of my wrongness. And so will he.

November 7, 1964

Sinclair Lewis turned down the Pulitzer prize, but accepted the Nobel.

William Saroyan turned down a Pulitzer prize, but accepted membership in the National Institute of Arts and Letters.

Ernest Hemingway, I have been told, turned down membership in the National Institute of Arts and Letters but accepted the Nobel, and accepted the Gold Medal Award of

Merit of the American Academy of Arts and Letters, of which the Institute is the parent body.

Boris Pasternak turned down the Nobel prize, but how much he had to say about that is anybody's guess.

And now Jean-Paul Sartre has turned down the Nobel. I wonder why.

I am not at all satisfied with the windy explanation he gave for his rejection of the most prestigious award in the literary world. He undoubtedly meant it when he commented that the Nobel goes only to Westerners and rebels of the East, that "the only Soviet work honored was one that was published abroad and forbidden in its own country." Sartre, though perhaps not a member of the Communist Party, has a record of devotion to it that will match any man's. Since his sympathies lie in that direction, he could hardly accept the Nobel if he believes that the prize is some kind of propaganda weapon against the Soviet Union and the Communist Party. If he had stopped there, it would be unreasonable to criticize him. On the same grounds he would have to reject the Laetare Medal of Notre Dame University, the Medal of Freedom of the United States government, and the Brotherhood Award of the National Conference of Christians and Jews—to name a few. He had already turned down the French Legion of Honor, and I suppose he would refuse an appointment as admiral in the Great Navy of the State of Nebraska, an honor which came to me ten years ago.

But Sartre did not stop with the explanation that the Nobel prize is used as a divisive device. He went on to say that "a writer must refuse to allow himself to be transformed into an institution"; he must not accept official awards because he would be adding the influence of the institution that crowned his work to the power of his pen, which "would not be fair to the reader." Now those are strange sentiments to come from a man who seems to pride himself on his independence. Does he want us to infer that if he had accepted the Nobel (or any other prize) he would have lost his independence? It would probably be unfair to Sartre to surmise that $50,000 and a gold medal are his price; and yet by rejecting the money and the badge he has very nearly admitted or implied that acceptance of the prize would destroy his independence. It seems to me that he is not very brave. He would have been much more effective as an artist and as a politician (though possibly ungracious) if he had taken the prize and continued to serve the Soviet Union and the Communist Party as devotedly as ever. As a politician, if not as a philosopher, he surely must realize that that course of action would be immediately and permanently more dangerous to the Nobel institution than his grumpy refusal has been. He could have taken the prize and said, *"Cela ne me dit rien!"*

I try awfully hard to be a constructive critic, but it is a fearful struggle. However, 1964 will soon be drawing to a close, and if I don't turn in some constructive criticism now, the year will go down as one in which I made little effort in that direction. I therefore suggest to the Swedish Academy that philosophers be given a prize of their own, distinct from the prize for literature. The Swedish Academy chose Sartre for his "authorship, which has always been rich in ideas and which has had a vast influence on our times, mainly through its spirit of liberty and quest for truth." That may be, and it may not, but Sartre's eminence is not so much as littérateur as philosopher. Is it desirable, you may ask, to keep them apart? Yes, it is. You could then judge the philosopher candidates without faulting them for their almost inevitably ponderous prose, and the literary candidates without faulting them for their not always faultless philosophizing. Then when our Swedish friends have established a separate category for philosophy, they might be persuaded to set up a separate one for poetry. There are so many subcontractors among the poets that they need a separate category; the metaphysical poets versus Robert Frost and Marianne Moore, for example, and the obscure versus the unclassifiable. Under the present catch-all system, the literature category provided prizes in successive years for T. S. Eliot, William Faulkner, and Bertrand Russell.

Say, Sartre, how come Russell didn't turn it down?

November 14, 1964

Television, we keep forgetting, is a business. It is conducted for the most part by a band of sharpies who differ from the old-time movie producers in one important respect: the TV boys went to college. They therefore can use words like empathy, dichotomy, and validity, which may puzzle the public a little but have the even more desirable effect of making the sharpies appear to be honest professors. The honest professor is a man who does not care much for money and who has not yet got a TV program of his own. I am not here to say that I prefer the unscrupulous, larcenous, vulgar man who made his pile in picture business; but at least he did not (because he could not) pretend that he was in business for your health, particularly your mental health. To some extent he was kept in line by the threats of fines in his own industry, by the fear of censorship, by nepotism—for the nephew he hired was just as likely as anyone else to knife him in the back. But to dwell now upon the sins and sinners of the movie era would be to use up space that I need for the TV people. We were all deceived and diverted when Mr. Newton Minow made his famous remark about TV. His intention, of course, was to characterize it as a wasteland in the cultural area. The immediate response to the remark was so favorable that it revealed an attitude that needed only a single word of expression. Wasteland. The right word at just the right time. Why, it even had a touch of T. S. Eliot (who forty years ago had made it two words), for the benefit of the intellectuals.

Unfortunately, the Minow epithet was so apt that it was

followed by a lapse into complacency. Through Minow we had told off TV, and we could now go on to something else. That, of course, was what the cooler heads in TV had anticipated. They, moreover, knew something else: that TV was a business, such a business! A friend of mine, father of a large family, was asked a few years ago how he coped with so many children. "Oh, we put them down in the cellar, throw them a few fish heads, and let them watch TV," he said. It doesn't spoil the story to tell you that my friend is a Harvard man; the captive audience that TV has is universal, and the sharpies know it.

They know that our capacity for indignation, as FPA was fond of pointing out, is negligible. The scandalous "$64,000 Question" and other quiz shows were defended by the sharpies, who showed that they had some capacity for indignation. The "so what?" attitude is a part of their morality. (Although they were among the ones who tried to inflict a national sense of guilt on the people when John F. Kennedy was murdered.) For months and months and profitable months they cynically cheated the public in as brazen a swindle as we have ever known, and I don't think they should be allowed to forget it. Nothing, really, has changed in TV. It is a business, and such a business!

I am a homebody who happens to have a long and wide acquaintance among men and women in the entertainment industry. I have also had forty years' experience in what has come to be called the communication arts, which is the flossy name for journalism, radio, TV, movies, and smoke signals. As a result of my associations, when I watch TV or listen to the radio, or go to the theater or to a movie, I see more than meets the eye. This does not make for an unmixed pleasure, especially when I have knowledge of the individuals involved in the production end of the things we see on TV. A good many of them went over the side when the movie business sprung a leak; some of them came from old radio and the theater; some from that breeding ground of talent, the advertising agency; and there are others whose origins are mysterious because they prefer it that way. But they have at last found a home. It is in that peculiar refuge known as The Box, and they have so quickly made it their own that I am dismayed at the prospect of ever budging them. They are the sharpies.

They are not all engaged in the task of putting out next week's western or tonight's version of Sidney Kingsley's *Men in White* or Sunday afternoon's examination into the incidence of homosexuality at schools of hairdressing. Some of them are on a higher, a policy level, and they're the ones to worry about. They are the ones who will try anything if it looks like money. They keep shows on season after season that benefit other sharpies, and when they want to get rid of a show they invoke the rating systems. I do not believe in the ratings, and I never will. I do not believe any figures that seem to indicate a public demand for reruns of Groucho Marx and Donna Reed. The one-man O'Hara Survey of a one-man audience, the only rating system I have found reliable, detected a trend away from Dinah Shore and Polly Bergen several years before the better-known polling organizations blew the whistle on those ladies.

November 21, 1964

Why, when we have all the evidence before us, do we persist in rejecting the Soviet Union's efforts to convince us that they mean business? As far back as I can remember, which is as far back as the czarist days, the Communists have been saying two things about business: they mean it, and they intend to put us out of it. Some of us accuse the U.S.S.R. of duplicity, treachery, and the whole catalog of sins against our version of honor. I recall that even those supreme chumps, the American Communists, went into a spin because Stalin had not told them that he was preparing to sign a non-aggression pact with Hitler. Twenty years later, we were horrified when Khrushchev said he would bury us, and again a little while later said that the living would envy the dead. Is it possible that our distrust of them is so deep that we do not believe them when they are being completely candid? It's possible, yes; but I'm inclined to doubt it. For almost fifty years now, the Russians have been stating calmly, threateningly, spontaneously, tactlessly, and always sincerely that they are going to win and we are going to lose. It has ceased to be a question of ideologies, of their kind of socialism against our kind of socialism. (They are abandoning theirs while we seem to be getting closer to it.) It is them against us, and they have never seriously pretended it wasn't. In a more peaceful context, they could be said to have behaved with admirable frankness. In any context, I think we have behaved with reckless naïveté.

As soon as I pause to get my breath, someone, who has been fidgeting all through the previous paragraph, fires this one at me: "All right, slob, do we go to war?" I'm ready for that one. The obvious answer is yes, we go to war when they are ready, and not one minute before. When they decide that propaganda, harassment, economic machinations, their expanding imperialism, and our own foolishness have taken too long, they will try something else. And if that doesn't work, if that doesn't put us out of business, they will shut off our water or stop our milkman or blow us all to hell. It is not their intention to triumph with a glorious military victory, to engage in valorous combat for the sake of their own morale. They have their own ways of stimulating morale that are more efficient and ruthless than ours. If they can gain their ends without knocking out a single token town, they will settle for that. And how do I know all this? Because they've been telling us so for half a century, and I believe them.

The trouble with discussions of this sort is that they usually end when one of the participants asks that question about our going to war. We agree that war is unthinkable, that modern war produces no victory, etc., etc., etc. But that's how we argue it. We think from a defensive position, essentially that of the protection of the fifty states; and short of the classic, all-out war we are a people who refuse to get deeply involved in semi-wars in remote areas, such as Korea and Vietnam.

Our psychology is not that of the British, a power that for centuries (centuries, let us remember, are hundreds of years) depended on the capture and policing of colonies. We had it all here, between the two oceans, and though we have fought our wars elsewhere, they were fought to keep intruders at a distance (except for that impertinent German submariner who fired a shot on Cape Cod in World War I). We have been comfortable where we are, and that kind of thinking is hard to change. I doubt if it was changed by Korea, and that's a bit of unfinished business that never bothered us very much. It is our kind of thinking even now, when a super-bomb can be lobbed over the North Pole. It has become an oddly Oriental, fatalistic way of thinking at a time when the Chinese have signed up for the nuclear games; entry fee, $5,000,000,000; winner take all.

But it is not the Russians' way of thinking. The Romanoff dynasty lasted little more than three hundred years, a cohesive if not a unifying influence. When the dynasty changed, in March, 1917, the Russians did not scatter. In a short while, as history is measured, they changed the machinery at the top and were back in business. Under the new management they have lasted nearly fifty years, and though the faces change, the ursine visage remains the same. The sound is the same, too. It is a warning growl.

We are a nation of men and women and children who visit our national parks, and paying no attention to the rangers and to the growls, are terribly disappointed when the bear chews someone's arm off. Comrade Armoff, I believe you.

November 28, 1964

If Barry Goldwater (or anyone else, for that matter) could hold together the 25,000,000 citizens who voted Republican on November 3, he would be a shoo-in in 1968. Goldwater did not start out with as many as 25,000,000 voters. He started out with a few thousand, as any and every candidate with the exception of Eisenhower has had to do, regardless of party. Willkie, for example, started out with a few small dinner parties in New York City. Dewey started with even less, prior to his election as governor. In 1948 Truman won with fewer votes than Goldwater got in 1964. In 1932 Roosevelt won with fewer votes than Truman got in 1948. You can do funny things with statistics, and one of the easiest things you can do is to ignore them. But you cannot ignore 25,000,000 voters who would stick together for four years.

As it happens, however, Goldwater's 25,000,000 are not going to stick together. As a unit they did the cookie bit, they crumbled, on November 4. I voted for Goldwater with no expectation whatever that he might win, but in the hope that he might poll a sufficiently imposing population vote to keep the Republican Party in business. If he had reached 30,000,000 it would have been a moral victory and he would have carried along enough governors, senators, representatives and sealers of weights and measures to make it a practical political victory as well. But the defeat was so nearly complete that there is not much organization left. This country is run from and by Washington, and the sixteen Republican governors out of a possible fifty are not going to make a very formidable array against the federal government. When the Republican governors go to Washington with hat in hand, they must not be too disillusioned if they come back bareheaded. That's politics. The Outs are out.

The party's disintegration will be worse before it gets better—if it ever does get better. A factor in this disintegration will be, unhappily, the meetings of party bigwigs for the purpose of assessing damage and planning for the future. The purpose is laudable, but what really happens in such meetings is that a large part of the time is expended in fixing the blame. And you can imagine how much blame there is to be fixed after the Republican campaign of 1964. They will begin and end with Goldwater himself, but Rockefeller will get his share, Javits will be given his, and so on with Scranton, Romney, Lodge, John Hay Whitney, Bill Miller, Leonard Hall, Charles Percy, Kenneth Keating, Clare Boothe Luce, and William McKinley. Why McKinley? Well, wasn't he the symbol of the kind of Republicanism that apparently cost the party the election? I expect nothing constructive to come of these meetings. The persons I have listed failed to agree to support their candidate in the midst of the campaign.

The professional politicians among them—Hall, Javits, and Miller—will undoubtedly make some optimistic mutterings about the congressional elections two years hence. Already I have heard such dreams. But I come from Pennsylvania, where politics is every man's second occupation—when it isn't his first. I covered my first political story forty years ago. I may not have qualified as the logical successor to such parliamentarians as Rayburn and Dirksen, but I learned that the professional politician must begin by getting the money. The money, of course, is for the party, but the professional politician *is* the party, is he not? He is not, as they say, in business for his health. Not even Medicare. He keeps things going between campaigns, and he must have money to do that. Therefore, he talks about things like congressional elections two years away. But I'm very much afraid that for the next two years we are going to have such a docile House and such an accommodating Senate that Mr. Johnson will hardly know they're there.

That will be one of the unfortunate results of the Johnson landslide. The conservative elements of the Republican Party will no longer carry any weight in or out of Congress. The Republican moderates offer no real resistance to the Democrats, and seem to take a great deal of pride in pointing to the similarity of their voting records. (You recall the truism that the 1932 FDR would have spurned the Eisenhower platforms as too radical.) The docile, accommodating Democrats will respond to the liberalistic challenge of the Republican moderates by giving them something to aim at. Like the moon.

I am not a sore loser. On election night when I saw Mr. Johnson on television, walking in the rain at Austin, I shouted, "For God's sake, don't catch cold!'

December 5, 1964

It seemed like such a good idea at the start. Instead of giving a little here and a little there, why not lump it all together at one time? Then you wouldn't be pestered all year long by this charity and that philanthropy, one coming right on top of another, the Red Cross appeal followed by the Fight Polio drive, the Fight Polio followed by the Anti-Psoriasis, Anti-Psoriasis Week followed by the local campaign of the Society for the Preservation of the George Washington Hitching Post, until every week from the first of October to the end of June was claimed by at least one eleemosynary enterprise. It was inevitable that the idea of the Community Chest would occur, more or less simultaneously, to various interested parties. It seemed to make good sense, and it had two features that we Americans find irresistibly attractive: it was Efficient, and it was Big.

Big it was, and no doubt about it. By writing one big check instead of a dozen small ones, Joe Blow could get the whole thing over with at once, and he didn't have to search for that reassuring line about tax deductibility. Efficient, and big. Merger, my sweet! What American can fail to respond to the merger pitch, with its practically guaranteed promises of efficiency and bigness? Flynn was never more in than the Community Chest.

But then Flynn—or you can say O'Hara, if you like—noticed that among the organizations that were more or less quietly getting into the act was Planned Parenthood. Now I happen to believe in birth control. It might even be said that during certain frolicsome phases of my life I believed in birth control as devoutly as I believe in freedom. Without the one I could not enjoy the other. On a higher, less hedonistic plane, the arguments in favor of birth control were sociologically and hygienically irrefutable, in my judgment. But many millions of my former co-religionists were forbidden to practice it. Never mind about how many did and did not practice it. The important thing here is that Planned Parenthood was offensive even to those who disobeyed the dicta of their faith by using contraceptive devices or methods. As a matter of fact, birth control was one of the points of difference between the church and me, as it has been with so many "fallen away" Catholics. It is curiously repetitive, then, that Planned Parenthood should be one of the reasons for my falling away from the Community Chest.

(You will forgive a slight touch of levity in this earnest discussion if I recall that in my Hollywood days there was a young actress who was known as the community chest.)

It seemed to me that the Planned Parenthood outfit did not properly belong among the beneficiaries of a charitable enterprise that was asking for contributions from men and women of all faiths. And I said so. Oh, you may be sure I said so.

I also said that the Parent Teachers group did not belong among the organizations that shared in the Community Chest. The PTA people and the League of Women Voters, which of course began with laudable purposes, have become a kind of joint committee for political action. Political action of the liberal-progressive persuasion. I do not favor the abolition of such groups, but they get none of my dough.

I gave the YMCA some money a couple of years ago, because they do good work and have been doing good work for fifty years to my personal knowledge. But the YMCA is a member of the Community Chest, and in order to give them some money I had to contribute to a special fund that was not required to divvy up with the community fund. I decided that this was too devious, so I have ceased to be a YMCA contributor, just as I have been compelled to withdraw my support of other organizations that participate in the community fund.

That left me feeling a bit like Scrooge at Christmastime. It is easy to reconcile oneself to feeling like, or being like, Scrooge the rest of the year, but a certain amount of controlled benevolence is more appropriate to the Yuletide. So last year I gave some thought to the matter. In the community where I have lived for more than fifteen years is a group of men who not only function twenty-four hours a day in line of duty, but also do the same kind of work with the young that I observed in the YMCA, and they do it in their free time. I am talking about the cops.

It may be evidence of my good behavior in these, my twilight, years that I have not made the acquaintance of the Princeton Township and Borough police. (It was not always so in other towns.) But it didn't take me long to find out that these are a pretty good bunch of men, on duty and off. The same is true of the cops in Quogue, Long Island, where I have passed the last twenty-eight summers. The point here is that in the two communities, 135 miles apart, in which I live the twelve months of the year, the cops are OK with me. That is why I give to the Patrolmen's Benevolent Association.

December 12, 1964

There is a story that during World War II, Winston Churchill complained to Franklin D. Roosevelt that the British were having trouble with Charles de Gaulle. De Gaulle was then in England as head of the Free French, and he was refusing to go along with the British on some policy matter. Roosevelt listened to Churchill's complaint and then said, "Who pays him?"

"We do," said Churchill.

"Well?" said Roosevelt.

"Ah, I see what you mean," Churchill is reported to have said. The British thereupon put financial pressure on de Gaulle and his followers, and the general had to knuckle under. Why not? He had no place else to go.

Some years later the young senator from Massachusetts, John F. Kennedy, visited Algiers and made some statements about Algerian independence that are said to have infuriated de Gaulle, as well they might. I can imagine the response here, for instance, if a French legislator should pay a quick trip to the Hawaiian Islands and there declare that the Hawaiians ought to sever their ties with the U.S.A.

Kennedy's unsought advice in Algiers is a matter of record; the "who pays him?" story is gossip, but I happen to believe it's based on fact. Both stories contribute toward a better understanding of de Gaulle and his attitude toward the British and us. If I were de Gaulle I'd feel the same way.

As it happens, I am not de Gaulle, although a lot of people think we look alike. (I think he looks like a combination of John Hersey and me.) Long before anyone noted any physi-

38

cal resemblance between the general and me, I began to admire him, and I continue to do so. He may well be the greatest patriot France has ever had, in the tradition that was established in our history by George Washington. The now conventional response to the word patriotism is to quote Dr. Johnson's remark that it is the last refuge of the scoundrel; but no one has succeeded in making a scoundrel of George Washington, even after two centuries, and the debunkers are going to have a hard time making one of de Gaulle. The Johnson remark is a handy bit of invective to have around when the occasion arises, such as the emergence of a Hitler, but between a Hitler and a de Gaulle, who is the scoundrel? Between Washington and Benedict Arnold? Between de Gaulle and Pétain? The fact is that de Gaulle has kept a good word in good standing, simply by being a strong patriot in the cause of La Patrie.

Our State Department and our volunteer diplomats among the journalists and TV personalities have created and perpetuated a profile of de Gaulle as an untractable enigma. He is, they say, difficult. You bet he's difficult! He has consistently refused to be jostled around by our boys at State and their often reluctant companions at 10 Downing Street and Whitehall. The expedient combine of State and the Foreign Office manages to convey the impression (with, I admit, a little help from de Gaulle) that he is a stubborn creature who doesn't know what's good for him. But he knows what's good for France, and he may even know what's good for Europe. Oddly enough, he is doing pretty much the same thing Pershing did in France in 1917, when Foch and Clemenceau wanted to use the AEF as replacements and Pershing insisted on keeping our army together. Pershing prevailed, and the war was won, but it would have dragged on endlessly if the French had been permitted to stick an American division here, an American brigade there, to relieve the exhausted French and British troops. Similarly, de Gaulle does not see France as a minor power, subject to the stratagems of the American and British diplomats. Therefore, he is stubborn.

But enigmatic he is not. Whether he is being difficult about the British membership in the Common Market or giving us trouble in NATO, he is almost totally predictable. On any question, all you have to do to first-guess de Gaulle is to ask what course is most desirable from a Frenchman's point of view. Not an Englishman's or an American's or a German's or a French internationalist's point of view, but the point of view of a highly principled French patriot. In 1939 I nearly lost a good friend, a Francophile, because I told him that France was a third-rate power that would not be able to stand up to Hitler "when the time came." I would not have made that assertion if de Gaulle, or someone like him, had been in authority. Once in a while a man will come along who compels your admiration and trust. George Catlett Marshall was such a man, in my lifetime. James Forrestal was another, and he was my friend. They too were described as enigmatic.

December 19, 1964

I have yet to read any of the books or plays of Gore Vidal, so for all I know he may be the greatest thing to come along since Virginia Woolf (whose name I always have to look up so I don't misspell it). I know so little of the Vidal writings that I would have to take your word for it if you said he was the greatest thing to come along since Jim Tully. My impressions of Vidal have been acquired by his practically unavoidable appearances in the press and on television.

A couple of years ago he ran for Congress against an incumbent woman, and she defeated him. (She was defeated in 1964, but by someone else.) Nevertheless he got to Washington at his own, not the taxpayers' expense; he is related somehow to Mrs. John F. Kennedy, and as a literary cousin he was forthwith absorbed into the In Group during the Kennedy Kultur Kick. Among his other distinctions, John F. Kennedy was the only President of the United States to ask me for my autograph, but that was while he was a senator. It was easy to forget that when he became President—and he forgot it. Therefore I was not an on-the-scene observer of the social-cultural activity at the White House, and I am full of regret. I played my last touch football about thirty years ago, and I have a bad back (Mr. Kennedy and I had the same therapist for a while), so all I wanted to do was sit and watch. That's all I want to do anyhow, but I knew I was missing something.

Just once I wanted to go to a White House party and be an onlooker, and eavesdropper, of a conversation participated in by Saul Bellow, Gore Vidal, and Stewart Udall, the Secretary of the Interior. I have to imagine Bellow and Udall and their fascinated silence as Vidal held forth, nonstop and with a warning twinkle in his eye to prepare them for the next good one that was coming up. He is so pleased with himself, is Mr. Vidal. In that respect, among other respects, he reminds me of a writer named Cleveland Amory, who is also pleased with himself. Vidal seems to enjoy what he is about to say before he says it, while he is saying it, and after he has said it. "Oh, that was a real good one," he seems to be saying. Amory's self-satisfaction is indicated by the way he returns his pipe to his mouth. He holds on to the bowl and nods in agreement with himself, frowning a little because his listeners do not always get the point. Actually they may have heard the point and the argument before; that often happens, as Amory is what might be called a rediscoverer of ancient truths, and when he is not retelling items from the Old Farmer's Almanac, he comes up with bits of society gossip that indicate at least a cursory reading of the late Maury H. B. Paul, the original Cholly Knickerbocker.

Vidal, Amory, and another writer named Louis Auchincloss are quite big on the book-and-author luncheon circuit. It is a long while since we have had three writers who are also well connected socially (Auchincloss went to Groton) to serve up to the ladies on a single platter. The ladies were probably getting a little tired of the same old John Gunther and William L. Shirer and chicken à la king, and the new trio may have arrived just in time. I imagine too that a lady feels more like dressing up for a Vidal-Amory-Auchincloss luncheon than for a feast of reason and skipped dessert that features James Baldwin and Dick Gregory. In their hearts, bless them, the ladies know that Vidal, Amory and Auchincloss are light.

The curious thing about Vidal, Amory and Auchincloss is the way they have inadvertently exposed the basic snobbism of the intellectuals. These three boys have made no secret of their social connections (my understatement for this week), and yet they are regarded as completely safe by the Adlai-Eleanor cult. It is true that with the various LBs in the White House the boys no longer enjoy that kind of prestige, but I have a suspicion that the intellectuals are going to be more faithful to Vidal & Company than to the Johnsons. We'll see.

December 26, 1964

Soon after accepting the call to this pulpit I promised that I would not try to change anyone's mind. If the force of my arguments and the clarity of my reasoning had a gently persuasive effect, that was all to the good. But as for attempting the hard sell, my natural diffidence restrains me. Someone in my family—I forget who—used to say that you attract more flies with honey than with vinegar, and that's a good thing to bear in mind the next time you wish to attract flies. Place a soup plate filled with honey, not vinegar, on the window sill, and when you have attracted a sufficient number of flies, let go with the DDT. I do not know how well the method would work on mosquitoes or wasps. That kind of experiment is better left to E. B. White, Donald Culross Peattie, and other nature-lovers, while we go on about the merits of the hard sell versus the soft sell.

It is a temptation to attempt the hard sell today, dear brethren. Sad to say, I have an unenviable record of failure thereat, but it would be gratifying if I could get 10,000,000 or 20,000,000 readers to bombard their congressmen with letters and post cards of opposition to the admittance of television apparatus in court trials and legislative proceedings.

On several occasions I have drawn fire and bottles of acid and whatever else was available when I have spoken out on this subject. Quite understandably, the television outfits have fought quite hard and a little dirty to discredit me and my efforts to keep the cameras and cables and crews and commentators out of the courtrooms and caucus rooms. I represent me and no one else, but CBS and NBC and the other outfits ganged up as though I had infinite resources behind me. The vilification and vituperation were so intense that I was astounded that one voice could be the cause of it all. I had said only what I believed.

But after the smoke of battle and the stink of the bombs had cleared away, I began to wonder a bit. Although I had spoken only for myself (in letters to one of the New York newspapers), the news and public relations departments at NBC and CBS responded with all their might, and it occurred to me that perhaps they knew better than I did that I was also speaking for a considerable body of public opinion. The television outfits are so big and so rich, and they are so easily intimidated by anything that calls itself a poll, that if they had any reason to believe that I was the spokesman for a large but inarticulate number of men and women, they had better fight back. And they did, and they were pretty dirty about it, and now they are once again trying to push their way into courtrooms and legislatures, and I would like to keep them the hell out.

For better or for worse, we have those cameras and microphones in ballplayers' dressing rooms and at airports and fires and massacres and fashion shows and testimonial dinners, and always with those mike-holders asking that same stupid, "How does it feel to?" question, whether the interviewee has won a beauty contest or lost three children in an automobile accident. That's the electronic age. But we can keep them out of the courtrooms, and we can keep them out of the legislative chambers, especially out of the courtrooms. Any professional politician will tell you that the real business of a legislature is not done on the floor, but in private offices, hotel rooms, and on unbugged park benches. But in judicial proceedings, where a man's life or liberty or property or reputation is at stake, there is no place for any kind of camera, let alone the apparatus that television requires.

Robert Sarnoff, chairman of the board of NBC, is the latest to sound off. He has the gall to declare that television "is now a basic part of the American press." Someone ought to tell him the basic meaning of the word press, if anyone can tell him anything. Television is no more a part of the American press than the movies are part of the theater or CBS is a part of the American League. As a member of the working press for more than forty years I refuse to accredit Sarnoff. One of the finest pieces of reporting I ever knew of was the job done by a man named Bill Ent, on the great fire in Pottsville, Pa., in 1914. He didn't have a pencil on him, so he made notes with a house key. Sarnoff and his people would need a two-ton truck, cameras, microphones, and a crew of six, and they still wouldn't get the story.

It was a dismal day for us all when the publishers thought there could be a peaceful coexistence of the newspapers and those mike-holders. But maybe we can keep them out of the courtrooms. We can try.

January 2, 1965

The Yale men at Yale are beginning to speak up. Thus far their murmurings and mutterings have not become a roar, and maybe they never will. Nevertheless the basic Blues are making themselves heard, which is an improvement over the long period of sullen silence.

Yale and Harvard are the national universities in the sense that Oxford and Cambridge are the national universities of Britain, and naturally you get all types at all four institutions. But over the years Yale has evolved a Yale type that hardly needs description. He is likely to be at least fourth generation, of part-Yankee stock, financially well fixed, conservative in all his tastes, friendly and polite without making many new friends after college, loyally but not unswervingly Republican, tolerantly but unwaveringly Protestant, optimistic, patient, dependable, and good. I have known hundreds of him, and it goes without saying that I like him. The things that I don't like about him relate to matters in which he differs from me, but I can be tolerant too.

The conservative tradition at Yale has required patience, but patience is a trait of conservatism. The basic Blues have needed more of it than other groups because their alma mater has been more subject to invasion and boring from within than other universities. The liberalist and his partner the extreme radical have nothing further to gain at the city colleges and most of the state universities. That battle has been won. And the liberalists and radicals have not wasted their time on the smaller, independent colleges, with their parochial prestige and woefully limited financial resources.

45

The big universities have been the target, and Yale, with all that money and prestige, has been under fire, so to speak, for three decades. Why hold up the candy store when the bank is just a few doors away?

I did not read the William Buckley book, *God and Man at Yale,* which was a Yale conservative's criticism of conditions at New Haven. But here was an almost perfect example of Yale patience at its worst. The basic Blues, of whom I am so fond, turned their indignation at Buckley, with the result that his book had the effect of screening the evils he attacked, while Buckley himself took the rap for saying anything at all. The basic Blues seemed to feel that Buckley was a nasty kid who had gone around telling people that Mama was misbehaving with the delivery boys. When the excitement died down, the delivery boys were smoking Dad's cigars and driving the family Jag.

Not to labor the analogy too much, it could be pointed out that the nasty kid had some older brothers who were doing absolutely nothing about Mama while the delivery boys were moving in. The Yale hierarchy—the professors and the chaps of the Yale Corporation—practically told the boys to use the front door.

But there are mutterings and murmurings. I was surprised to discover, in private conversations and in the pages of the Yale alumni magazine, that there was a great deal of resentment when Martin Luther King was given an honorary degree. (Yale was the first major university to elect a Negro captain of football in the person of Levi Jackson.) A Yale faculty member spoke out forthrightly against the visit of a couple of anti-American Soviet poets. (Predictably, a Columbia professor insisted that the anti-American Russians had every right to speak at Yale.) There was even a certain coolness a few years ago when the then President of the United States, Mr. Kennedy, was given an honorary degree and took that occasion to speak rather patronizingly to and of the business community as represented by the basic Blues. Mr. Kennedy had begun his collegiate career at Princeton and transferred to Harvard, so it was easy to kid the basic Blues for having been bypassed. But they did not like Kennedy or his speech.

The remarkable thing is the patience of these men, especially as they see the university they loved being taken away from them. It is almost a handicap to have gone to Yale if you want to get your son into the freshman class. I know of one fifth-generation Yale man who had to send his son to another Ivy League university. The son got his degree at the second choice, so he was not a complete moron, but Yale would not stretch a point to maintain a tradition. Alumni will tell you that that sort of thing happens all the time. If it happens often enough, Yale may lose alumni financial support. Then, as they say in Wall Street, the university will have to "go public."

January 9, 1965

I have always believed that Senator Joe McCarthy was the most surprised man in the country when so many people began taking him seriously. He was a third-rater, to give him all the best of it, who stumbled upon a few pieces of information that were potentially dangerous to some individuals in or near the government. He then, according to my theory, got carried away with his personal publicity, and thereafter there was no stopping him. He would say or do almost anything for publicity, and when he was not saying or doing something awful, his frightened enemies in or near the government were getting the publicity for him.

In a strange, madly ironic way he may have contributed to the election of John F. Kennedy to the presidency. As a man of Irish descent and a Roman Catholic, McCarthy had been the target for the anti-Irish Catholic feeling that has always been strong in this country. McCarthy became a convenient symbol of the Irish Catholic, and when it became fashionable in and out of politics, but especially among liberals, to attack McCarthy, it also became safe, or safer, to get in a few licks on the Irish and the Catholics. He brought out the Kluxer in all sorts of individuals: Racquet Club types, Jews, moderate Protestants, first-generation and tenth-generation stock. He seemed to bring out the Kluxer in everybody but the Kluxers themselves. But when this disgusting orgy of know-nothingism was over, it could not be repeated so soon again when Kennedy ran.

(Perhaps I ought to reveal my guilty secret: my maternal grandfather was born Israel Delaney. He was a convert to the Roman Catholic faith, but all his antecedents back to pre-Revolutionary times were just one Protestant after another.)

McCarthy has never been to me very convincing as a major villain. You cannot make an epic heavy out of a man who combined the rascal and the chump and not much else. I attended some of the Army-McCarthy hearings in Washington, and during a recess Senator W. Stuart Symington, whom I have known for thirty years, came over to say hello to me. McCarthy had a terrible time trying to figure out who I was, and I saw him ask one of the other reporters, who didn't know either. Finally he did get me identified by a reporter who knew me, and on his way out he spoke to me. I burst out laughing, and McCarthy's cordiality vanished. At that time I had a page of my own in *Collier's*, a magazine which he read, and I really believe he thought a friendly greeting would win me over.

What he could not know was that I had just been thinking of an evening in Washington in 1934, when I was having dinner alone in the Grill Room of the New Willard. Suddenly out of the elevator came a couple of hoods with their hands in their pockets, followed by one man, who was followed by another couple of hoods. The man who walked by himself was Huey Long, and obviously the others were his bodyguards. Too obviously. The whole party reminded me of a Warner Brothers gangster movie, and I burst out laughing then too. One of the hoods came to my table and started to mutter angrily, until Huey Long, who was also laughing, called him off. Long knew exactly why I was laughing. McCarthy would never have known. Huey Long had the makings of a major villain; McCarthy was only the liberals' nightmare. With the help of Freud we could have studied that nightmare, but it's a bit late for that now.

As a nation we have not produced many major villains. We have had our share of scoundrels and cads and crooks and rascals. But we were not yet a nation when Benedict Arnold operated; we were a British colony, no more American than Bermuda or Canada. John Wilkes Booth was a psycho, and anyway the assassination of Abraham Lincoln, though a villainous act of major proportions, does not make Booth a major villain any more than Lee Oswald's loathsome act qualified him. Al Capone qualifies, but in spite of his Brooklyn upbringing and his Chicago hell-raising he was essentially an Italian, therefore not a home-grown major villain. Under that rule, Charley Luciano is also disqualified. Under present-day laws some of our financial and industrial giants of the 19th Century would be in the sneezer, but even our Supreme Court has not yet got around to tampering with the ex post facto laws. We do much better with our heroes, especially our military heroes, from George Washington to George Marshall. The fact that the American Revolution was run by the gentry, or nice people, has quite possibly had some enduring effect on us as a people. In my opinion we have maintained an average of about sixty-five per cent Good, or more good than bad. As long as McCarthy remained an inconspicuous slob he belonged with the sixty-five per cent.

January 16, 1965

One of the most difficult decisions a conscientious man has to make is the choice between pro and con on the subject of off-track betting. Another tough one—already disposed of by the voters of California—is whether to be for or against pay TV. These are only two of the problems which are complicated and confused by the arguments on both sides by men of good will and men of greed. On most controversial topics I know where I stand, but on the subject of off-track betting I confess that I vacillate.

The most powerful argument against off-track betting is, of course, based on the paternalistic fear that Mary Jones, housewife, is a compulsive embezzler. If the state should open up betting parlors in residential neighborhoods, Mary is going to take the family cash and visit the legalized bookmaker on her way to the supermarket. The result will be that on some days she never gets to the supermarket, and the Joneses once again dine on peanut butter. I happen to like peanut butter, and there was a period in my life when I was glad to have it to dine on, but it can get monotonous.

One of the more interesting aspects of the argument is the notion that it is the wife, the woman, who is going to blow the family bankroll on ill-chosen horses. Presumably, Dad is too busy at the office or the plant to nip out and get down three deuces across the board in the third race at Aqueduct. Nearly always the slave to the betting habit is depicted as the young housewife, the Betty White type who is wholesome, loyal, and true, but unable to resist the call of far-off bugles sounding post time. As it happens, I have been married three times, and each of my wives has enjoyed on-track betting, but as neither wife has been a Betty White type, my observations may not be worth much.

For whatever they may be worth, however, I submit them. A decade ago, while studying conditions in Reno, Nevada, I was amused and then appalled by the prevalence of slot machines in supermarkets and other retail establishments and by the addiction of housewives to the devices. Not only the Betty White types but the Marjorie Main types and the Carol Burnett and Donna Reed and Bea Benaderet and Shirley Booth types were developing their biceps at the coin machines. It was not merely a matter of getting rid of the loose change that remained after the housewife made her purchases. Again and again the girls would go back with folding money and have it broken into quarters and halves.

From having been pushed away from the combination windows at tracks all over the country, I have learned to respect the determined women bettors. I am forced to conclude that this eagerness will not diminish if the state legislatures legalize the neighborhood horse parlors.

But I cannot get too agitated over the possible effect on the housewives' morals, disastrous though it may be. Any surburban or small-town cop will tell you that daytime drinking among housewives is on the increase. There are also reports of other forms of hanky-panky, a more or less undesirable by-product of the new leisure. If the womenfolk have more time to get into trouble, the safer course for me is to let them police each other, and I'll stay out of it. My responsibility, if I have any, is to blow a feeble whistle on the girls to let them know that some discretion is indicated. They have somehow managed to create a national image of themselves as industrious little homemakers, who spend a large part of their time comparing detergents and cough medicines, and worrying about Dad's grouchy stomach. The opponents of off-track betting, on the other hand, have been trying to retouch that image. They would have us believe that Mary Jones, housewife, is a larcenous creature with an irresistible urge to get her husband in debt, undernourish the wee ones, and neglect the split-level, ranch-type cottage called home. Instead of those pleasant gatherings at the laundromat and the dutiful meetings of the den mothers, Mary and her friends will have daily sessions of horse-players. They will have neither the money nor the energy for the bowling alleys. The dough and the enthusiasm will all have been dissipated in the betting parlors, where the action is.

I'll tell you what does worry me, though. What happens to all that money when it comes under the control of the politicians? When those babies get their hooks on it, watch it go. You have seen how easy it is for them to divert highway tolls into nonhighway projects.

January 23, 1965

One explanation for the fact that a husband and wife who have been married a long time begin to look alike is that they eat the same food. It isn't my theory, and as an explanation it is not unassailable. But it surely has some merit, and I have been thinking about it in another connection. Using it as a point of departure, I have been working on a theory that people who feed off the same clichés very soon begin to think alike.

Two years ago you hardly ever heard anyone say, "In terms of . . ." Today it is inserted into all kinds of public utterances by all kinds of people, from Dean Rusk to Sammy Davis Jr. The other night I was listening to one of those gab programs on the radio. This one had five participants, including the moderator. In an hour's time the gabbers touched upon various problems, from unidentified flying objects to birth control, and no one was at a loss for an opinion. It is true that they tramped on each other's lines, and not all of the group always talked about the same thing at the same time. Consequently the listener soaking in a tepid tub and more relaxed than the gabbers was not always able to follow the dialogs. It is fair to say that the experience was like getting tuned in on two radio stations on the same wave length. Montreal and Moscow, for example. You get three people talking all at once—one of them talking about conception and another about perception and the third taking exception— and the mind wearies of the effort to stay with one gabber or another. But I was able to keep track of the gabbers' solo parts, and I found that each and every panelist said, "In terms of . . ." at least once.

I am not saying that all the people who cling to the same clichés arrive at the same opinions. But in a startling number of cases they depend so much on the clichés that what they say sounds like what their friends say, and the result is a uniformity of expression that implies a uniformity of thought.

My subscribers may recall that the word "valid" (along with its half-brother "validity") had a ten-year run that now seems happily concluded. "Valid" was as inescapable in conversation as "Volare" on your car radio, but "Volare" was easy on the ear and "valid" was offensive. It was so badly misused that people often said "valid" when they really meant nice. You got it everywhere, in book reviews and political talk, and I once heard a woman refer to Adlai Stevenson as a very valid person. Well, according to Webster's Collegiate Dictionary, one of the definitions of "valid" is "capable of being justified," but I'm sure that's not what she meant.

"Valid" got some stiff competition from "ambivalent," "dichotomy," and "accommodation," to mention a few. Among intellectuals word-dropping is as valid as name-dropping, and among politico-intellectuals you were nothing, absolutely nothing, if you did not drop that word "accommodation" into every conversation. It is still not quite dead as a substitute for "appeasement" and "compromise." It is a State Department euphemism for that word made so horrid by the late Neville Chamberlain, and it has come in very handy in our dealings with Cuba, Vietnam, Indo-China, France, Brazil, Venezuela, Chile, Canada, and fifty or sixty other countries that have to be accommodated. That's one cliché that seems to have influenced our foreign policy; I wonder what we'd have done without it. But it never quite caught on as "valid" did.

I believe that "in terms of" is going to be hard to get rid of. The phrase has an elusive quality that makes it hard to pin down. It is not a modifier, as "valid" was. It can be slipped in anywhere. At Christmastime I heard a kid say, when asked about his vacation plans, "Well, in terms of going away, I'm thinking of going skiing." When I was that age we prefaced every statement with, "As a matter of fact," and as a matter of fact I guess that holds all records for long-distance meaninglessness. In the '20s the In Group—by which I mean those of us who had coonskin coats—were heavy users of the word "whereupon." We stuck in "whereupon" every chance we got, but "whereupon" is a narrative word and its use was somewhat curtailed.

One expression that I could worry about, that has caught on among the young and not so young, is "Forget it!" Boy, could I write a sermon about that! In terms of valid accommodation, naturally.

January 30, 1965

My license as a merchant of opinions will be lifted unless I get something down on paper about the Great Society. But I have a good excuse for my tardiness. Instead of dismissing the program as the political rhetoric I believe it to be, I had a look at a book called *The Making of Society*, which was edited by V. F. Calverton and includes chapters by Plato, Aristotle, St. Augustine, Machiavelli, Adam Smith, Mill,

Paine, Proudhon, Darwin, Spencer, Pareto, Veblen, Dewey, Strachey, Marx, Lenin, Trotsky, Hitler, Mussolini and other social philosophers. Some of the book was unreadable, as is often the case with writings about the most interesting subject in the world—the human being. The bloodless profundities of social philosophers and historians are often due, I think, to the fact that the writers forget that they are writing about men and fall into the error of writing about Man. It is perfectly all right to write about Man if you want to, but when you do you cease to write about men. You might just as well write about Apple, or Horse, or War, or Peace. You restrict yourself to general statements about apples and war, or you write about a condition called Life and a lifeless symbol called Man.

And yet it is not the philosophers' inhumanity to man or the professors' insistent displays of scholarship or the dictators' remoteness from their victims that repels me. It is the rediscovery, in *The Making of Society,* of the giant intellects' lack of respect for knowledge. There is not space here to review the book—it would need more space than the book itself—but it can be said that at least a dozen times the writers of *The Making of Society* indicate that they know all the right answers. Knowledge unachieved is obviously so much greater than the little we know that the enormity of our ignorance ought to produce constant humility, especially among the men who know something. Not so, however. Here, for instance, is Aristotle: "As I have already shown what sort of life is best, in my popular discourses on the subject, I think I may very properly repeat the same here . . ." Aristotle died in 322 B.C., and as I had last read him forty years ago it surprised me to find that he would be quite comfortable in the John Birch Society.

Here, for instance, is the Marxist economist Werner Sombart, whose *Socialism and the Social Movement in the 19th Century* was still being published in 1924: "Only one who chases after the phantom of a world republic will be able to imagine a social development outside of national limitations." Sombart died of natural causes in 1941, but such heresy could have got him liquidated under Khrushchev. Sombart brilliantly predicted the creation of the Common Market—but without predicting World War II or the other factors that contributed to the desirability of the Common Market.

I could go on, but Aristotle and Sombart—the immortal and the comparatively obscure—typify the heavy thinkers' positiveness and lack of humility. There is plenty more documentation of both characteristics in *The Making of Society*.

In the making of the Great Society we are to be led by a man who has been President of the United States for more than a year, but whose chief concern during most of that time appeared to be the November elections. Now that they are good and out of the way he seems to be the most uncomfortable occupant of the White House since Warren G. Harding. Parodying O. O. McIntyre, the late Ring Lardner once wrote: "One-word description of Franklin D. Roosevelt. President." It would never do as a description of Mr. Johnson, who has dropped a twenty-year plan into the legislative hoppers, called it the Great Society, and probably will refer to it from time to time when he remembers to. Undoubtedly he saw an advance copy of the vice-president's speech to the joint meeting of the AFL-CIO leaders, which was most reassuring to Big Labor. Predictably Mr. Johnson will have things to say to steel management when the time comes, and they will be less reassuring. Congress will be asked to spend a lot of money on education and on our friends and nodding acquaintances abroad, and the culture consultants will come up with a couple of successors to Grandma Moses and Robert Frost. Lumping all these and many more heterogeneous items, the administration will be able to say that the Great Society is a fait accompli.

Three years hence, with another presidential campaign in full swing, the Great Society will be the label for all the things the administration wants to brag about. And that, my friends, is just about all the Great Society ever will be. I say that, of course, in all humility.

February 6, 1965

According to ancient Chinese lore, if you saved a man's life you assumed the responsibility for his well-being throughout the remainder of his days. The idea behind the custom was, of course, that if you had not interfered, the man might be enjoying heaven.

How rigidly the Red Chinese adhere to this belief is impossible for me to say. The Marxist fundamentalists would probably reject it as humanistic, humanitarian nonsense. Despite my Japanese-sounding name, I am so completely western in my point of view that I have never quite accepted the notion that you must go on supporting a man whose life you have saved. But in a subtle and insidious manner the notion has been spreading like tamefire, which is slower than wildfire but eventually just as destructive. It certainly seems to be one of the few enduring and durable items in the foreign policy of the United States of America. Our open-handedness to the British and French during the past fifty years of peace and war has been so steady that for most of that time it has been taken for granted by the French, the British, and by us. In dollars and cents (cents!?) it has become so enormous that I am told it is impossible for even a congressman to get a straight answer from State and Treasury as to how much the British and French owe us. Maybe State and Treasury don't know the answer. The arithmetic is probably staggering in more ways than one. If they do know the answer, they're not telling, possibly to save us from becoming embarrassed at our own generosity. It would be nice to know, though, just to be able to reply when a Frenchman or an Englishman tells you that the Yanks joined them in 1917 and 1941 when most of the dirty job was finished. Even if they were right about that—which they are damn well not—we ought to be able to remind them that between 1918 and 1941, and between 1945 and this very day, our peacetime assistance has been nothing to sneer at, so stop sneering. The Chinese coolie whose life you saved was not instructed to sneer at you while accepting your lifelong subsidy. That was definitely not part of the Chinese custom.

Some of our open-handedness was expedient, militarily or diplomatically, and is to be regarded as the cost of war or the price of peace. With that there can be no quarrel. But when the money is being handed out to help needy people or nations, we ought not to be made to feel that we are scoundrelly chumps. We cannot buy respect or affection, wholesale or retail. In this naughty world good deeds are not always rewarded with gratitude or acknowledged politely. But they ought not to be received with contempt. A grant-in-aid is not a kick in the teeth.

The decline of good manners is fairly universal, and not limited to great nations or teenagers. The massacre of medical missionaries is only one dramatic example of resentment against those who give. A hard-up nation takes our money on condition that there be no conditions. But our own institutions of higher learning do precisely the same thing. The halls of ivy resound with the cackles of fund raisers who have conned alumni and friends into giving money without strings. Just give the money and never mind asking what it is to be used for. If you plan to hand over $1,000,000 to alma mater you no longer have much chance of knowing how the money will be spent. If alma mater deigns to accept the money that you contribute for a specific purpose, you or your heirs may have to go to law to enforce the conditions of your gift—and you'll probably lose. The money you leave to establish a scholarship fund for, let us say, young men and women who were born in your native county, may end up as salary for a group of research professors who are not teaching anyone anything but are writing books that oppose everything you ever believed. If it takes an act of legislature to divert your benefaction, it won't be the first time. The man who would like to honor Aunt Elizabeth with a dormitory named for her had better stay alive until the broomstick is on the roof. Otherwise construction may be postponed while the university argues in court that the dormitory money should be used for something else. And if that same man is so foolish as to believe he has any right to make any suggestions about the architecture of the dormitory, he is in for some more disappointment.

The irony today is that so many large gifts are made with the thought of the tax advantages they provide. The rich Joe reasons that if Old Siwash or Old Yale doesn't get the money, the government will. But the benefactor may find that he has endowed a project to study ways and means to relieve him of whatever he's got left.

February 13, 1965

The arrival at my house of a pair of shoes from England and the departure from this earth of Sir Winston Churchill occurred in a twenty-four-hour period. Nothing could be easier than to relate the two events to each other and to our time.

The shoes came from Peal & Company Ltd., and were preceded by a form letter: "The Directors of Peal & Co. Ltd. announce with regret the closure of their Bespoke workshops as of January 1, 1965, due to the ever increasing difficulty experienced over the last few years in obtaining skilled labour to replace their long serving staff who have left due to retirement and deaths. It is very distressing to have to close down this side of our business that has been under control of Directors in direct lineal descent of its founder for 173 years." So, in part, went the letter.

As I have been a Peal customer for thirty of those years and had ordered my shoes last fall, I now am not quite sure whether to wear them or have them bronzed. Yet I cannot imagine my daughter saying, "And these were Daddy's shoes, that he gave himself for his sixtieth birthday." So I guess I'll just ignore sentiment and wear them, hopeful that I may last as long as they do.

Even the magnificent Winston did not last forever, in spite of the preservatives of cognac and cigars. I never met him, and never particularly wished to. There are men whom you admire, respect, and even feel some affection for without wanting to get any closer. They are public men, and unless you go to see them for a specific purpose, a professional interview, you are wasting your time and theirs. They relax only in the presence of other public men, of equal prestige. (Too many people in journalism too easily deceive themselves as to their relationship with these public men, and quickly forget that it is their journalistic credentials and not their personal charm that makes them useful and acceptable to the bigwigs. Offhand I can think of only one journalist—Joe Alsop—who has the social qualifications and aplomb to carry him through a nonprofessional evening with the Churchills or the Roosevelts, and to get him invited to such an evening in the first place.) But a man who lived so much of his long life as a public figure, and who did so much writing of one kind or another, provides an accurate if incomplete picture of himself. Churchill was the last imperial Englishman, in the best meaning of the epithet. His empire was first of all England itself, where no one in his time quite measured up to him, and in the dominions overseas and the rest of the world he came to represent English guts, English ethics, English honor, and English intelligence. Many another Englishman combines these attributes, and those who do produce a type, than which there is no better in the human race. You knew that when he said Englishmen would fight in the streets, he meant that he would be there with a Webley in his hand. You likewise knew he spoke truly when he told our Congress that if his father had been an American and his mother English, instead of the other way round, he might have got to

Congress on his own. He could have been President, as easily as he could have been a member of the House of Lords. He did not like to lose but he knew how to lose. He was a good hater, too.

His aristocratic ancestry served its only useful purpose: it made him absolutely sure of himself. When he made mistakes, which in his position tended to be disastrous, he could remind himself that being a Churchill was not of itself a guarantee of omniscience. Life rebuked him on various occasions, but because he had guts and principles and honor and intelligence, it took ninety years to wear him down. And after all, he lost to chemistry, as we all must. He could weep, but he did not cry himself to sleep.

I shall not weep over the closure of my English bootmakers' Bespoke workshops, but you will hear no peals of laughter. Winston Churchill, one of a kind, passes out of the picture—probably wearing Peal shoes. Peal, after 173 years, will make no more shoes to order, and I am left without an extravagance. Good men and good things vanish. In the case of Peal shoes, no one will suffer from their disappearance; but we will all suffer, and don't think we won't, from the disappearance of the kind of craftsmen who made the good shoes good. In the grave new world of Bop and Pop and automation there will be no customers for the handmade article. I don't see any new Churchills on the horizon, either.

February 20, 1965

It used to be fun to watch the power struggles in the motion-picture industry. Cousin against cousin, nephew against nephew, executive against brother-in-law, brother-in-law against outsider. You would hear that Morrie was on the way out, then would follow weeks of trying to guess who was on the way in. You would see long lines of Cadillac limousines parked outside the adminstration buildings until well into the night, then shorter lines of some of the same limousines parked outside the Beverly Hills and Brentwood residences of the competing vice-presidents. Then, a few days later, the face-saving announcements in the trade press as Morrie was stripped of all real authority and his contract settled for a hundred cents on the dollar.

Large sums of the stockholders' money were involved in these payoffs to the incompetent, but since it made no great difference to the human race if the whole motion-picture business slid into Santa Monica Bay, the parochial or family disputes within the industry had only local significance. Such is not the case when the individuals concerned are in charge of running the country, and the country happens to be in most respects the most powerful in the world.

We have survived quite a few spells of bad relationship between the President and the vice-president. Indeed, as you look back from the present through to Coolidge it almost seems as though the relationship creates bad feeling between two men who, ideally, should be mutually respectful and admiring. John Nance Garner was sixty-three years old, thirteen years older than Roosevelt when they were elected, and did not expect to become President through Roosevelt's death. He was merely sitting out the four years with his old cronies and his whiskey and branch water, and keeping more or less to himself his opinions of the New Deal. Henry Wallace was more useful to Roosevelt and the New Deal because he was a New Deal zealot, but FDR and Wallace were an association and not a partnership. Roosevelt was afraid that Wallace would go too far, and Wallace was afraid that Roosevelt would not go far enough.

I now believe that Roosevelt was so sick and so weary that he would have accepted Truman's old haberdashery partner as his running-mate in 1944. In any event Truman and Roosevelt were not together long enough to develop the antagonism that characterizes so many President–vice-president relationships. It is no use speculating how long it would have been before FDR felt he had to slap Truman down, but I have no doubt some chastisement would have been inevitable.

The least gracious of all was of course Eisenhower in his treatment of poor old Nixon. The standard explanation for the opposition to Nixon is that he "rubs people the wrong way." He does, and no doubt about it, but I know some of the individuals who rub Eisenhower the right way, and between them and Nixon, I'll take Nixon. I did. I voted for him in spite of Eisenhower's reluctant acknowledgment of Nixon's existence during and prior to the 1960 campaign. I wonder how many times Nixon must have said to his wife, "If he doesn't like me, why doesn't he get someone else?"

The absence of camaraderie between Kennedy and Johnson is too recent to need restatement now. Mr. Johnson lost no time in expressing his approval of the legislative victory of Mayor Wagner's boys over Senator Kennedy's boys, and that shows where Johnson stands in relation to the Kennedys. But even more timely is the President's refusal to send Mr. Humphrey to the Churchill funeral. I cannot quite believe that Mr. Johnson feared that through force of habit Mr. Humphrey might take his place behind Prince Philip of Edinburgh and give out with that Humphrey grin. I can only believe that Mr. Johnson did not wish to have Mr. Humphrey play President on his time.

The comical situation is not comical at that level, where

simple incompatibility of personality can quickly become serious distrust. Truman, you recall, did not know about the A-bomb until it was very nearly time to order its use. It does not appear that Johnson would impose much more confidence in Humphrey. To some degree that kind of relationship is unavoidable under the present arrangement. I therefore in all seriousness propose that the office of vice-president be abolished.

Congress is having discussions about what to do in the event the President becomes critically ill or goes off his rocker. I say get rid of the vice-presidency first and then go on to legislate the line of succession. The lawmakers know where to reach me if they require my assistance. I shall try to be helpful.

February 27, 1965

Adlai Stevenson and Rafik Asha could have timed it better. Adlai Stevenson is the former governor of Illinois, the former candidate for the presidency of the U.S., and currently the chief U.S. delegate to the United Nations. You all know who Rafik Asha is.

You mean to say you don't know who Rafik Asha is? Well, he just happens to be the Syrian ambassador to the UN, and he is the man who blew the whistle on a New York cop who he claimed had been rude to him. It seems that Rafik, who enjoys diplomatic immunity, had double-parked his car, and that the cop made some cracks about diplomats and their abuse of privileges. If you have ever seen those UN cars blocking traffic, or speeding up Park Avenue on their way to a cocktail party, or parked in front of a fire hydrant, you would be sympathetic to the cop. But Rafik made an official squawk and the cop was transferred to Harlem. In fourteen years on the Police Department the cop had never had any disciplinary action against him, but that made no difference. We have to be nice to the Syrian ambassador to the UN and to all the 114 other ambassadors to the UN and all those drivers of UN diplomatic cars.

Mr. Stevenson's double misfortune was that just before the Asha matter was made public he, Stevenson, lectured the New York Police Academy on being nice to UN diplomats. At almost the very moment that Stevenson's lecture was being shown to the Police Academy on closed-circuit TV, our embassy in Moscow was under attack by a mob of Commie hoodlums. The Moscow police stood and watched while 740 windows were smashed, ink bottles pelted at the embassy, and the American diplomats virtually imprisoned in the building. There is no record—and there won't be any—of a Moscow cop's being banished to the Moscow version of Harlem, although the U.S. government made its official protests against the attack on the embassy. The attack was so well conceived and executed that the dismounted Cossacks had only to act in a supervisory capacity.

Attacks on American embassies and American officials and American citizens have gone on unrestrained and unpunished for years. They are the consequence of a quasi-official policy, instituted by Henry Wallace and Eleanor Roosevelt, and continued through later administrations, which amounts to over-concern with what foreigners think of us. The debilitating effect of this policy has been that we became the only non-isolationist, non-nationalistic power in the world. In the process we have been abandoning the habit of taking a stand, so that when we do attempt to take a stand, we are not sure how it's done. Kennedy, you say, took a stand in the Cuban crisis—but where was Adlai Stevenson on that one?

We take a stand, or seem to be taking a stand, in Vietnam. Mr. Johnson sends a man called McGeorge Bundy (what a name for a comic strip) from the White House to Vietnam. Bundy is one of Johnson's top men, and Southeast Asia is supposed to take heed. Bundy returns to Washington, and before he has had time to unpack, a Vietnam barracks is bombed and thirty Americans are killed. That is what foreigners think of us and our stand.

We did, of course, take one firm stand. Our mighty nation managed to subdue a hundred-pound woman, Madam Nhu. Guided by the representatives of TV and the press, our government put her out of action, although she happened to be on our side. This was our only triumph so far, but I'm afraid it is not quite a solid enough base on which to start rebuilding our national pride.

Maybe we have no pride left. Well, that's not true. The most remarkable and the only encouraging phenomenon to come out of Vietnam has been the courage and perserverance of our airmen and soldiers. They do not seem to realize that gallantry and guts are going out of style. They are proud of their deadly, dangerous work, but it is too much to hope that this small band of men can inspire the young or embarrass the old. Churchill's few, to whom so many owed so much, are as dated as Thermopylae's Spartans. True, one of these men was given the Medal of Honor and photographed with Mr. Johnson, who is never without his little enameled ribbon of the Silver Star (I still don't know what Mr. Johnson got it for). After the ceremony the airman vanished from the public view and what remains is Mr. Johnson with all his problems, Mr. Stevenson with all his problems, his excellency the Syrian ambassador to the United Nations with his dignity restored, the ink stains on the American embassy in Moscow, a blank space on the wall of the American embassy in Prague, where another mob tore away the Great Seal of the United States of America. That last item came in as I was writing. I don't think I'll wait for more.

March 6, 1965

Almost the only place for a man of great wealth to retain his perspective, to be able to live as a human being, is in government service. This is a fact which is overlooked by the citizens who say, "What does Nelson Rockefeller want in that rat race?"

A man as rich as Nelson Rockefeller has a choice among several lines of endeavor. He can take an active interest in the family business and make more money; he can dedicate his life to the fleshpots; he can make a career of saving the whooping crane; he can perfect his golf game until he can consistently beat Arnold Palmer and Mysterious Montague; he can sit around for thirty or forty years while trying to make up his mind what he wants to do. Or he can enter government service, as Rockefeller has done.

Nelson is the only Rockefeller brother whom I have not met, and the only one I ever worked for. In 1942 for a brief time I had one of the longest titles in the government: Chief Story Editor of the Motion Picture Division of the Office of the Co-Ordinator of Inter-American Affairs. I served WOC— without compensation—so I never got a paycheck with that title on it. My immediate superior was another rich man, John Hay Whitney, but he wisely left to join the Air Force, and I left to become a spy. I could tell some lurid tales about my career as a secret agent, but none of them would be true. I never even met the head man in the Office of the Co-Ordinator of Inter-American Affairs, who was Rockefeller.

But I have had my eye on him for a long time. The study of enormously rich men is more than a hobby with me. It is an occupation that can be almost as entertaining as girl-watching, and in a surprisingly large number of cases you can do both at the same time. The classic dialogue on the subject of rich men was the one between F. Scott Fitzgerald and Ernest Hemingway, in which Fitzgerald is said to have remarked that the rich are different from the rest of us, and Hemingway to have replied, "Yes, they have more money." But I have always felt that Hemingway's line rated better as flippancy than as observation. You do not, in the United States of America in the 20th Century, so casually disregard a man's power to put his hands on a billion dollars.

So much money affects the owner of it and both ends of his relations with other people. The billionaire who wants to obtain or achieve something without buying it must either possess some special skill, or work in some line where the whim of purchase is not the deciding factor. I would be the last to say that money does not play an important part in public elections, but money alone no longer can swing it.

Thus Rockefeller has acquitted himself rather well in making a career of government service, especially in running for elective office. I don't like him, but his father was an estimable citizen who began his good citizenship at home, and some of his goodness seems to have rubbed off on his sons. The pathetic figure that was Edsel Ford illustrated the kind of demands that were made on the character of John D. Rockefeller Jr., but Rockefeller was equal to them. John D. Rockefeller Jr. did not submit to the tyrant who was his father, nor to the potential tyranny of five sons. Considering all his advantages, Nelson Rockefeller turned out better than most, and by no means are all the returns in on him yet.

This, however, is not concerned with politics as such, but rather with the rich man in political enterprise. To a man like Rockefeller, it must be literally engaging to be governor of New York State. To use a word that has become almost meaningless, it is a challenging job. No man alive is rich enough to pick up the tab for the expenses of running the State of New York, so the governor, though he may be a billionaire, is compelled to ask small men of small means to provide his administration with the money to foot the bills and to make him look good. It must be a splendid and

chastening experience for a multimillionaire to have to ask
relatively poor men for money.

It must also be a humbling experience for a rich governor
to find that the grand promises he made to the taxpayers are
no more substantial than if they had been made by the
lowliest assemblyman. That is one way to learn perspective.

March 13, 1965

One night at a party at the home of my friends and neighbors, the J. Robert Oppenheimers, I found myself in conversation with an amiable gentleman named Oswald Veblen.
That, I should say, was in my drinking days, when my
natural shyness used to vanish with the coming of night. The
fact that Dr. Veblen was the author of *Invariants of Quadratic Differential Forms* and of *Foundations of Differential
Geometry* was formidable but not overwhelming. After all,
was I not the author of *Pal Joey*?

We got on the subject of Education, which admittedly was
somewhat more in his line than in mine, but I had some
thoughts on the subject. I had a theory, which I propounded
to Dr. Veblen, that most men and women get very little out
of college, and that instead of taking the courses offered on
the college level, the students would be better off if they
were to repeat the four years of high school. My argument
was that there were millions of high school graduates who
had passed trigonometry, Virgil, French or Spanish, and been
given their high school diplomas, but were unable to do plane

geometry, translate two lines of Caesar, or order a meal in a modern language. Why not do a four-year review of the entire high school curriculum, in the hope that the second time around the students might really learn.

Veblen agreed patiently that a man who really learned all the things he had been taught in high school could be considered a well-educated individual. He also agreed that most people got so little out of college because they had not learned what they should have learned in high school. "Aha," thought I. In almost but not quite the immortal words of Lyndon B. Johnson, I had Veblen in my pocket.

But before I was able to get too pleased with myself, Veblen said, "But what about the students that did learn the first time?" We had only to look around the Oppenheimers' living-room for proof that there were many such persons. Indeed, it was altogether possible that in that company I was the only person who could not at that moment have passed all the examinations of all the subjects studied in high school. And incidentally, I had been valedictorian of my prep school class.

Veblen's question demolished my theory, which was never going to get very far in any case. But I picked up the pieces and put them together again. The cracks still show, the theory is no sturdier than ever. Nevertheless it has some value, and as we are about to commence spending and squandering billions of dollars on Education, let us hope that some of the money will be earmarked for teaching and learning. At least a million dollars will go toward those nonrepresentational sculptured animals in the schoolyards, and a few million more will be needed to install floodlights on football fields so that students getting credit for Band will be able to practice marching. In France there is a rather violent campaign on to demand salaries for students. The little jerks wish to be paid to go to school, and in 1965 the most remarkable thing about the campaign is that the French thought of it before we did. (Apropos of which, my friend Veblen's uncle wrote an overestimated book called *The Theory of the Leisure Class.*) Somewhere, sometime, a few bob ought to be appropriated for the study of teaching and learning.

It is nonsense, it is rot, to say that school is harder now

than it used to be. I checked the college entrance requirements for Princeton University in the Class of 1915. The dean who helped with my research was so astonished by the requirements that he said, "If it was that tough now, we'd be out of business." The students at Caltech and M.I.T. are no more typical of the 1965 high school graduates than the Oppenheimers' dinner guests were representative of the Jet Set. We have always had Caltech and M.I.T. types, and now we have more of them because we have more of every type. We have many, many more illiterate, semiliterate, and uneducated graduates of high schools. They are the product of the educational progressives and of automatic promotion and of the high incidence of incompetence and ignorance among schoolteachers on all levels.

I understand that the president of Yale has a motto on his wall which reads: "Better Salaries for Teachers." What ever happened to Lux et Veritas?

March 20, 1965

It did my old heart good to see Julie Andrews give Jack Warner a swift kick in the pants, and to do it so gracefully, so graciously that Warner was not quite sure what hit him. Miss Andrews, of course, did not actually give Warner the boot. All she did was to thank some Hollywood correspondents for an award and to thank Warner for not giving her the lead in the movie version of *My Fair Lady*, thus making it possible for her to get the award. You would hardly call the Andrews speech a new deep in subtlety, but Warner is not celebrated for his sensitive perceptions, and subtlety would have been wasted.

An actress who goes by the name of Maureen O'Hara took it upon herself to rush to Warner's defense. At least she indignantly insisted that everyone loved Warner. But though I seem to share a surname with Miss O'Hara, I do not share her belief in the unanimity of affection for Jack Warner. Moreover, Miss O'Hara (formerly Fitz-Simon) carelessly revealed that Warner Brothers is her home studio, and such an admission may have caused some onlookers to remain unconvinced of Jack Warner's popularity.

A week or so later a second and more substantial rebuff was administered to Warner when the Academy Award nominations were made public and his substitute for Miss Andrews, Audrey Hepburn, did not get on the ballot. Characteristically, a sorehead, or write-in, campaign was begun in behalf of the Hepburn-Warner ticket. The campaign, which is going to cost someone a lot of money, is almost certainly not going to be paid for by Walt Disney or 20th Century-Fox. And yet someone is going to have to pay for it. If as many people love Jack Warner as Miss O'Hara seems to think, the cost may not be too high; but if Mr. Warner wants to be on the safe side, he ought to be prepared to spend about $10,-000,000. He has it, of course. He needs it.

Already the campaign is under way, and one of the explanations for Miss Hepburn's not getting the nomination is that people found it difficult to believe she was altogether convincing as a Cockney guttersnipe. According to this argument, Miss Hepburn is so ladylike, if not so downright regal, that the audience resists her impersonation. Now that never would have occurred to me. She is thin almost to emaciation, and therefore believable as an undernourished London slum girl. Then later on in the story, when she has been taught how to speak good English and to mind her manners, she ought to be just perfect. To me, at least, she has always looked and talked like an actress who went through a refinement process. As I was touted off the movie *My Fair Lady* by my personal movie-taster, I cannot say how convincing she was as the graduate of the 'Enry 'Iggins Finishing School. In the stage version Julie Andrews was superb, but Jack Warner bought the movie rights and he probably prefers actresses with long necks.

It has not been a joyful month for executive types. Jack Warner had to face a mutiny, and a man named James Aubrey was deposed as programing head of CBS-TV. Aubrey was known in TV circles as The Smiling Cobra and as Jungle Jim, and inferentially was not as revered as Dr. Schweitzer. Of course he may have got those nicknames from TV creatures who were no less ophidian than he. The field of television is so full of cobra types that at a safe distance it may look like a bed of tulips, swaying in the breeze to the music of that former oboe player, Mitch Miller, playing "Tiptoe Through the Reptiles."

Aubrey, a Princeton man, was immediately succeeded by one John Schneider, a graduate of Notre Dame, who apparently has not yet acquired a nickname. I know what it is to be "schneidered" in the game of gin rummy, but that term was not inspired by Aubrey's successor. (It may, of course, be revived and given a slightly different meaning after Schneider has gone to work on next season's CBS schedules.) My favorite uncle graduated from Notre Dame about sixty years ago, and in his memory I have been somewhat resentful of the insults to his alma mater in that Goldfarb movie. However I know nothing about Notre Dame today, and am unable to say whether the communication arts have placated the university by putting an alumnus in charge of programing at CBS. If Eugene Augustus Delaney were alive today it would be my guess that he would regard Schneider's promotion as hardly more than a step in the right direction. But Uncle Eugene was a mining engineer, with different standards. Like, say, the difference between drilling and chiseling.

March 27, 1965

When my father, as a young physician, first hung out his shingle on Tchoupitoulas Street, New Orleans, Louisiana, he would kill time by shooting rats on the levee with a Flobert rifle. That was in the last decade of the 19th Century. A short while later he moved back to Pennsylvania and acquired four good shotguns for hunting quail and pheasant and rabbit. He also had a .32-caliber revolver, which he often carried on night calls. When I was about ten years old he bought me a Winchester .22-caliber repeating rifle, and I set up a range in the cellar. My father was a good shot with the scatterguns, and I wasn't bad with the rifle. Both my grandparents owned firearms. One grandfather was a captain in the Union army and fought in numerous campaigns with pistol and saber. One of my uncles was good with shotgun and rifle, and hunted the woods of Pennsylvania and Canada. I own half a dozen firearms, some sporting and some for protection.

The above brief history of three generations of firearms in one family could be duplicated 50,000,000 times. At least 50,000,000 times. In the sixty-two years from 1901 to 1963, between the assassination of McKinley and the assassination of Kennedy, it would be impossible to say how many American families have owned firearms, but 50,000,000 is a conservative estimate. Nearly every farmer in the land owned a shotgun, and many farmers owned shotgun and rifle. In the small towns where I grew up, the fathers of my acquaintances on all economic levels owned revolvers or pistols. You could go to just about any hardware store and purchase anything from a Daisy air rifle to a .30-caliber rifle that would stop a bear.

In the autumn of every year of those sixty-two years the woods were invaded by men and boys bearing weapons of various degrees of firepower, which they handled with varying degrees of skill or a total lack of it, with a varying sense of responsibility or a total lack of it. A careless youth with a .22 would kill a man a mile away without being aware of it; a stupid man with a 20-gauge shotgun would kill a Jersey even though she had "COW" plainly printed on her back. The usual word for the hunting season was slaughter, human and animal, while the careful gunners groaned.

At other times throughout the years men and women committed acts of violence and crimes involving firearms. Men and women on occasion used firearms to commit suicide.

And so on.

No one has ever argued that the firearm is not a potentially dangerous apparatus. What else is it intended to be? We buy firearms, and have been buying them throughout the life of this land, because of their lethal capacity, for food and for protection. Their use as a means to provide food is minimal, but in 1965 they are once again resuming their early indispensability as protection. The crime rate is up, and a Chicago judge has just decided that a hoodlum with a broken bottle in his hand is less dangerous than sworn officers of the law, a decision which is not going to make life in Cook County any less precarious.

The man who more or less by accident now occupies the White House likewise has been parroting the chant of the anti-firearms campaigners; he lends the prestige of his office to the argument that John F. Kennedy was murdered with a mail-order rifle and that therefore private citizens should be disarmed. I do not know where Leon Czolgosz obtained the weapon that killed McKinley, or Zangara the gun that killed Anton Cermak instead of Franklin D. Roosevelt, or John Schrank the revolver that pinked Theodore Roosevelt. But I do know this, Mr. President: Lee Oswald learned to shoot while a private in the U.S. Marine Corps, and I do not regard that as an excuse for disbanding the Marines. Oswald used a telescopic sight, so must we stop grinding lenses?

Oswald was a Communist sympathizer who spent considerable time in the Soviet Union, but when he assassinated Kennedy we did not attempt to assassinate Khrushchev.

There are already so many weapons in the hands of criminals, and the courts have been making crime so much less hazardous for them, that there is in effect an active discrimination against the law-abiding citizen. How long do you suppose it's been since Lyndon B. Johnson has entered Central Park at night? And how long since he has allowed Lady Bird to walk a few blocks on Fifth Avenue in the evening unescorted?

April 3, 1965

This column is now six months old, which makes it something less than an institution, but is a long enough time to make possible some sort of inventory.

It got off to a good start. Two papers that signed for it in advance were not at all pleased with my early efforts, and told the syndicate that unless I wrote to their liking, they would not sign on again at renewal time. The editor of one of the papers—a journal of the liberal persuasion—seemed to believe that his threat to cancel would be enough to make me change my ways. When I read his letter to the syndicate, I said, "Release him right away. Tell him to go to hell, and don't wait for renewal time." That was done.

Since that time other papers have dropped out, others have signed on, and I have been having a ball. So much so, indeed, that I have often been tempted to change to a daily or thrice-weekly column instead of the present schedule. But I am writing a long novel, and that takes it out of you; four or five hours at the typewriter every night is only part of the task. The hours away from the typewriter, with the problems of character and construction and technique to be dealt with, make the writing of a weekly column a relaxing interlude. Also, in all possible modesty, I am aware of the fact that there are competent columnists besides myself, but not too many good novelists. So the writing of these weekly messages, and the response to them, are a pleasure and a luxury.

What I knew in my heart has been confirmed: that this country contains a considerable constituency of confused and concerned men and women who are leaderless and feel lost. They are the non-kook conservatives, who have never questioned, for instance, the Negro's right to vote, but who refuse to accept the guilt that the liberals try to splash all over non-liberals. They—we—distrust the distortion of interstate commerce laws by which the federal government is arrogating to itself more and more powers that were clearly not intended for it. The active or complacent cooperation of the Supreme Court in all such matters has made Monday, the court's decision day, a day to be dreaded. Monday can be bad enough without those hebdomadal announcements that the Supreme Court, in its infinite wisdom, has opined that the fathers of this country did not mean what they seemed to mean. Blackball a man from your club and he goes gunning for the club's liquor license, thereby proving that your instinct to blackball him was proper, but putting the club out of business nevertheless.

The non-kook conservative wonders, for instance, about the abolition of capital punishment. Who says capital punishment is not a deterrent to murder, and who could possibly tell how many murders and assassinations have been deterred by the fear of the consequences? The non-kook conservative wonders about fluoridation of the water supply, punitive taxes on cigarettes, socialized medicine, cheating in exams, and the outrageous scheme to combat the increase of narcotics addiction by making the stuff easier to get. He wonders what really happened at Yalta and Potsdam, and why, and what is happening in Vietnam and why. He wonders why we can do so much for the steel industry of India, but do next to nothing for our own railroads.

All these and other matters are disturbing to men and women who are the non-kook conservatives in all sections of the country. This nation is so big that generalizations about the American people as a people are unsafe, but there is a body of opinion not restricted to sectional or economic or social status that seems to be waiting for a leader who may never come. It is a body of opinion, but it is otherwise unorganized, and though it is numerically larger (I am convinced) than various pressure groups, it is ineffectual against the organized minorities.

What these people need is a man who believes as they believe, who is vigorous and articulate and courageous, who is so incorruptible that he will not settle for one of those bipartisan sops that the administration may throw his way when he begins to get somewhere. If such a hero exists, my guess is that he will have to make his presence felt first and that organization will follow, rather than the other way around. In the six months that I have been at this post, I have learned for certain that people are desperately eager to follow such a man. Waiting for Righty, you might say.

April 10, 1965

It was a frightening picture that has stayed with me, and I am not one of those who use that word frightening every day.

The taxi drivers of New York City had refused to be organized into a union. Back in 1934, for instance, the drivers had to fight the goons who overturned their cabs and beat them up, but the hackies remained unorganized. So it has remained until this year, and the professional unionists did not like that. There are only 11,000 cabs in the city, but they are a public conveyance, and the public had a constant reminder of the fact that in all these years the unionists had been unable to compel the hackies to join up. From the professional unionists' point of view, that was a disgrace, and it could not continue.

So this year the unionists went all out. Although there had just been a fare increase, that made no difference to the unionists. They began working on the hackies early in the winter, finally calling a meeting in Madison Square Garden, which was attended by several thousand hackies. To make sure the meeting would be attended, the unionists announced that the hacks were not to roll that day. Some did, and their tires were spiked, windshields were smashed, some members of the public and some hackies got hurt. At meeting time the hacks were not rolling.

The head of the electrical workers' union said it did not matter if some people got hurt. What mattered was that the hackies had to come into the union. The head of the garment workers screamed and waved his arms and said his union had 180,000 members who would support the hackies, and he emphasized the word *financially*. The mayor of New York, who will run for re-election this year, sat there with the head of the electrical workers and the head of the garment workers, and thereby gave quasi-official support to the takeover. The mayor is not personally popular with the hackies, but the garment workers and the electricians are big unions and he needs them.

You looked down at the first few rows in the audience, and you saw the new breed of professional unionists, who obviously had never driven hacks for a living. And interspersed among them were the union tumulers. A tumuler is a cheerleader, a master of ceremonies. It is a Yiddish word that used to be applied to the entertainment directors at the summer hotels in the Catskills. Danny Kaye, for instance, started out as a tumuler. But Willkie had his tumulers at the

Republican convention in 1940; Goldwater had them. Hitler had them.

The meeting ended, and the unionists had won. After all those embarrassing years of shame, all they had to do was smash a few cab windows, injure a few citizens, spike a few tires, and get Van Arsdale of the electricians and Dubinsky of the garment workers and Wagner of City Hall on a platform, and the hackies succumbed. You can buy beer at Madison Square Garden, but this was not even a beer-hall putsch.

Well, not quite. But it's the way you get your message across if you want to organize the recalcitrant. Some violence, a large quantity of inconvenience to the public, the promise of financial support by Big Labor, and the active cooperation of compliant politicians.

A few days later Martin Luther King demanded a total economic boycott of Alabama industry, and did he not state that he would enlist the support of the unionists? Had he not already been photographed with another Detroit boy, Walter Reuther? Had not various governors sent their representatives to Selma? The naïve, the outraged, the victimized, the men and women who loathe the Ku Klux Klan seem to join with the exhibitionists, the subverters, the sinister, and decent indignation reinforces the new fascism.

We are looking in the wrong direction for the new fascism, which will not be called fascism and will not be identifiable by swastika armbands. The Hitler-Mussolini kind began in beerhalls and in marches, among middle-class people who were more or less committed to some form of socialism. We saw what happened to them, and to the rest of the world in the process. The word Socialist remains in the official title of the U.S.S.R., where fascism seems to flourish. The socialism which Eisenhower saw creeping into our system of government is now inherent to it (with some help from Eisenhower himself). The latent evil in goodness is not always apparent. Cancer is the life force gone wild.

April 17, 1965

A small beef with Yorkshire pudding has been issued by Prince Philip. (The Pope issues a bull; the prince issues a beef.) According to the Associated Press, it is the prince's lament that he cannot go to a movie or drop in at his local pub without being bothered by autograph hounds, people nudging each other, and all those irritations that accompany fame.

Concurrently, Roger Maris, the home-run king, has been accused of taking a poke at someone in a night-spot. Without knowing anything of the circumstances, I am inclined to side with Maris. I do not like people who get into fights with ballplayers and instantaneously announce that they are bringing suit against them.

But to get back to Prince Philip, his predicament, if you can call it that, could not have come as any great surprise to him. He will have been married eighteen years next November, as time flies, and he surely must have known that marriage to a member of the British royal family might entail certain sacrifices along with the benefits and perquisites. His father-in-law was not in the best of health; we all knew that. The king-emperor did indeed pass away five years after Philip's wedding, and Philip's wife became queen. We all knew that well in advance of its actual occurrence; when a king dies, the next in line gets promoted, and Philip knew that. On the eve of his marriage, he had been created Duke of Edinburgh, Earl of Merioneth and Baron Greenwich, also a Knight of the Garter, and given the style of H.R.H. These honors were conferred on him by the king himself, therefore

Philip had been given a strong hint as to what sort of life he was in for.

At the time of his marriage he was twenty-six years old and had been an officer in the British Navy with the Mediterranean Fleet and the British Pacific Fleet for six years. During that period he may have acquired certain tastes and habits that pass unnoticed among commoners but are not generally regarded as suitable for royalty, and he was already a member of Greek royalty, by birth. He was, in fact, extremely well connected among various European royal families, but as a junior officer in the R.N. he probably could drop in on the latest Nova Pilbeam or Douglas Fairbanks Jr. movie without attracting attention. Also, since he is not a startlingly unusual man as to looks, I imagine he could go to a saloon and have a mild-and-bitter, and nobody would bother him. In wartime especially hardly anyone gives a second look at a junior officer.

But the fun of impulsive visits to the cinny for a viewing of the latest Ronald Squire and Margaret Rutherford film, and the casual pink gins at the nearest saloon bar, had to be abandoned by the prospective bridegroom of Princess Elizabeth. Then when the marriage had taken place and there were all those trips abroad, and offspring to look after, and coronations and weddings and christenings of children and aircraft carriers, and polo and fox hunting and more trips abroad—Philip was kept pretty busy. Perhaps therein lies the explanation for his delayed nostalgia for the humble pleasures. I have no way of knowing. A year or so ago I met the man who is the new British ambassador, but I would not think of taking up his time with such a conjectural question. Besides, he might not know the answer, and that would be embarrassing. So for the moment we must be satisfied with my theory that until now Prince Philip has had so little time to himself that he did not miss the movies and the pubs.

Now, however, Britain has a Labour government, and Labour can always be counted on to make rude noises about the cost of maintaining a monarchical anachronism. Some Liverpudlian is sure to squawk at the cost of pipeclaying the Horse Guards' gauntlets and the electric light bill at Buckingham Palace. This would be the right time for such complaints; it might divert the citizens from Labour's boo-boo in accusing the U.S.A. of irresponsible use of the same poison gas that Britain has been using all along. In any event, so long as a Labourite is at 10 Downing Street, royalty has to stay more or less out of sight. The big show is, you might say, in winter quarters, out of action until the next election. Meanwhile Prince Philip probably has plenty of time to go to the movies and drop in at the Crown & Scepter for a pale ale. He needs no excuse to watch a movie if Sir Alec Guinness is in it. Guinness is good for you.

April 24, 1965

Although I was not made unhappy by the defeat of James Roosevelt for mayor of Los Angeles, my feelings could not be described as exultation. James, it is true, did not exactly lay it on the line: he campaigned while keeping a tight hold on his job as congressman, and thus he lost what he did not have but kept what he had. His defeat, therefore, did not send him back to private life—if you can possibly imagine a Hyde Park Roosevelt having a private life.

Perhaps if the Los Angeles voters follow up their rejection of Jimmy's candidacy with a refusal to send him back to Washington for his seventh term, there will be substantial reason for real rejoicing. But let it not be premature. Jimmy lost out on the citywide count; he might not lose in the 26th Congressional District, which he represents and has represented more or less steadily since 1954. One of the truisms of political life is that you pick your spots, which is why an Englishman sometimes runs for office in a "safe" district that may be 200 miles from his native heath. The 26th_California may be a permanently safe district for Jimmy Roosevelt.

It is such a long time since I lived in California that I have not kept up with the mayoralty situation in Los Angeles. Roosevelt was beaten by Samuel W. Yorty, the incumbent, and I know very little about Yorty except that he opposed the election of John F. Kennedy in 1960. It would seem, though, that Yorty has the right stuff in him, but don't take my word for it. Opposition to the Roosevelts and the Kennedys does not automatically make a man a statesman, although it is a point or two in his favor. Yorty was a congressman before he was elected mayor of Los Angeles four years ago, and Jimmy Roosevelt wanted to follow Yorty from the House of Representatives to City Hall, and maybe have another crack at running for governor of California as he did in 1950. It would have simplified matters to conduct a gubernatorial campaign from the Los Angeles City Hall rather than from Washington, D.C.

Franklin D. Roosevelt Jr. has an assistant secretaryship in the Johnson cabinet, and there are mutterings that Elliott Roosevelt, the brigadier, is in politics in Miami, Florida. (Elliott, by the way, describes himself in the 1960-61 Who's Who in America as "writer and rancher," a combination that could make a man a successor to Zane Grey, but in this case hasn't.) Aside from the fact that he is a fellow member of a small club that I belong to, John Roosevelt does not impinge upon my consciousness. But the other three keep popping up in the public prints, usually but not always in some political context. In this year of grace a Roosevelt can still get his name in the paper, but the magic has been passed on to the name Kennedy. At political rallies the orators intone "John——F——Kennedy" as they once chanted "Franklin——D—— Roosevelt."

Theodore Roosevelt's sons never made as big a splash as their father, although they made pretty good newspaper copy. His namesake, Ted, was in fact a charming man whose heart, I thought, was never in the political activity for which he had a ready-made name. He ran for governor of New York in 1924 and was beaten by Al Smith, as he should have been, inasmuch as Al Smith was the best governor New York has ever had, and Ted Roosevelt was more ideally equipped by experience and inclination to become a white hunter in Kenya Colony. After Al Smith beat him, he was apparently content to lead his own life, and when his time came he died like a man. He had done his duty to his name, and he died doing his duty to his country.

Ted Roosevelt was never under the pressure that was exerted upon the sons of FDR. From 1932 on it got worse and worse. I was living in New York City most of that time, and night after night I would see the treatment they were getting from restaurant and night-club owners and cops and taxi drivers and ordinary citizens. People made fools of themselves over these young men. It was much more unsettling than if they had been royalty. In Britain, at least, it is not considered good form to gawk at royalty at play, but in our democracy men and women were obsequious, seductive, and insulting to the younger Roosevelts. I saw them, in the beginning, trying to take it in stride, but that was asking too much, because it went on too long. I am just as tired of them as anyone is, and I make no excuses for them now, but any final judgment of them must take into consideration the extenuating circumstances. They were victims of unearned fame no less than they were its beneficiaries.

May 1, 1965

A favorite topic in this pulpit is the demand for conformity among the liberals. The liberal who commits the slightest deviation from the line is subject to censure, abuse, castigation, and even banishment. Complete and absolute conformity is required of the men and women who join this movement that so proudly boasts of its nonconformist character. To belabor the obvious, there is nothing very liberal or nonconformist about the liberal nonconformists, nor is there anything new about this observation. It has always been so.

Nevertheless there is always some amusement and comfort to be had when a new case is added to the liberals' record of illiberalism. From now on you may expect to see less and less tolerance of the lost sheep of Independence, Missouri. As far as the liberals are concerned, Harry S Truman has had it. He will be damned from here to eternity, the piano player and captain of Battery D. And as is the custom when the liberals have to second-guess on a man, they must now set out to prove that they never really trusted him. At this very moment they may be going through his papers in an effort to compile a dossier that will offer proof that he had lunch in the Senate restaurant with Joe McCarthy, and was more than polite to Senator Eastland. He will not be able to deny that he was on speaking terms with Russell and Byrd, and just let him try to get out of those Confederate army ties in his ancestry. If they don't try to prove that Harry Truman was secretly soft on the Ku Klux Klan, my name is Hugo La Fayette Black.

Oh, Truman is in for it. The funny thing—and it is funny—is that he knew exactly what he was doing. He came to New York to accept a plaque from an organization called Freedom House, which is one of those black-tie groups that give plaques to former Presidents of the U.S. and other such deserving parties. They have a big dinner at the Waldorf at I-don't-know-how-much a plate, and presumably they pay the honored guest's travel expenses, which gives the h.g. a chance to see his grandchildren if they happen to be living in New York. In the course of the evening they say a lot of nice things about him right to his face, and everybody can be home and in bed by 1 A.M. As the Irish say, it's better than a poke in the eye with a sharp stick.

Mr. Truman arrived in New York a day or so before the big dinner, and as always he went for one of his daybreak strolls, on which he is invariably accompanied by newspaper reporters and the TV pests with their microphones and cables. You can see he enjoys these walks, on which he sets a pace that men a third his age have a hard time maintaining. Most of all he enjoys giving flip answers to the reporters' and TV mikeholders' questions.

On this occasion he was asked what he thought of Martin Luther King. He obliged by telling what he thought of Martin Luther King. He thinks King is a rabble-rouser, that the Selma marchers were show-offs, and that the demonstrators are not helping the cause of civil rights. When a reporter protested that King had been given the Nobel prize, the former President said, "He didn't get it from me."

Truman knew exactly what he was doing. He was in town to get a plaque from an organization that probably considered giving the plaque to King and then thought better of it. My guess is that Freedom House had planned to have King as guest of honor, but got cautious when King announced his boycott of Alabama. Freedom House is a nothing, really, except for its annual dinner, and if King continues to regard himself as a dictator of national policy, his presence on the dais of a Freedom House dinner might easily make it the last dinner the organization ever had. Pursuing my guess, I can believe that the Freedom House people decided to wait and see what King does this summer, and if it isn't too outrageous, invite him to the dinner next year. In the meantime, a former President of the U.S. is always a drawing card.

But someone had to go and ask Truman what he thought of King, and it got in all the papers and on TV, and it spoiled the party for a great many ticket-buyers. A columnist on the *Herald Tribune*, who has fashioned himself into a combination of Brendan Behan and Jimmy Cannon, was so outraged by Truman's remarks about King that he accused Truman of being old.

Well, Truman is old. He is eighty-one years old. But he is not as old as a man of thirty who is afraid not to conform. In 1948 I voted for Truman, and now I'm rather glad I did.

May 8, 1965

One of the least credible characters in John Steinbeck's novel *East of Eden* was a Groton trustee who secretly owned a chain of houses of ill repute. I have known many Grotties and, by marriage, am related to a few. Their general average for probity is fairly high and would be higher but for the fact that one of the most arrogant crooks in modern Wall Street history was a Groton boy. He was a crook, but he did not own a chain of bordellos. Steinbeck's insistence on a Groton trusteeship for his character was capricious and unconvincing.

However, life can always be depended upon to mirror art. An author can invent a character or a situation that is not acceptable in realistic fiction, then real life comes along and imitates it or tops it. Although I do not believe that there are any prostitution tycoons on the Groton board, I cannot deny that Yale University is a beneficiary of the television program *Peyton Place*. This news does not top Steinbeck's fiction, but in that Yale Blue Heaven Up Above, where William Lyon Phelps and Henry Seidel Canby may meet every afternoon for tea, there must be some embarrassment. Assuming that Harvard men also go to heaven (Princeton men go back to Old Nassau), I fancy that they are having a little fun with Dr. Phelps and Dr. Canby on the subject of *Peyton Place*.

Apparently Yale bought 70,000 shares of stock in the American Broadcasting-Paramount Theaters corporation, and in a year's time Yale has become $2,000,000 richer on a capital gain. Since it is ABC that presents *Peyton Place*, Yale has shared in the prosperous TV production of the Grace Metalious novel.

Now I am glad to see Yale or any other private university make a lot of money through private enterprise. I am fearful of the trend toward federalization of our educational system, and if Yale can be made safe by the profits of *Peyton Place*, so be it. One of the television outfits approached me last fall (after *Peyton Place* caught on) with an offer to do for me what ABC had done for the Grace Metalious estate. I declined the offer. But perhaps if I had been persuaded that by letting TV dramatize one of my books I would be contributing toward higher education, I might have consented. My relations with higher education have not been too cordial, but if I were convinced that a TV dramatization of one of my books would save Harvard from total federalization, we might work something out. Some of my best friends went to Harvard.

I should imagine that Harvard would make its first pitch to James Gould Cozzens because he is not only the author of *By Love Possessed* but also a genuine Harvard alumnus. I am one of many authors who admire Cozzens's work, and I would not stand in his way if he were disposed to initiate a program to save Harvard. But Cozzens makes his home in Williamstown, Mass., and they have a college there. When Sinclair Lewis lived in Williamstown the college ignored him, possibly because Lewis was a Yale man, although I am only guessing on that. I live in Princeton, N.J., and am not a Yale man, but official Princeton University has ignored me as Williams did Lewis. I have no information on Cozzens's relations with Williams, but if Harvard's most distinguished living author is to be wooed by his alma mater, it had better look into the situation. It would be just too awful if Cozzens were to save Williams instead of Harvard.

It is perhaps an exaggeration to say that the late Grace Metalious has saved Yale. Nevertheless her posthumous support has been considerable, and she did not even go to Yale. She was widely read by undergraduates and alumni, that much I can testify. For every mention of the writings of William Lyon Phelps and Henry Seidel Canby that I have heard in the past twenty years, I have heard ten mentions of *Peyton Place* by Yale men. Make that twenty. Oh, make it thirty. It is fitting, therefore, in the light of the popularity of *Peyton Place* among Old Blues, that the dramatization of the novel should turn out so happily for the Yale bank account.

More significant for higher education in general is the potential income-producing factor of popular authors' works on TV. It is probably too late for Princeton to negotiate with Mickey Spillane, as the Mike Hammer series was all sewed up years ago. But there are other uncommitted authors. On the secondary-school level there is, of course, Louis Auchincloss. He went to Groton, and don't you forget it.

May 15, 1965

Some of the faithful have been writing in to ask why I have failed to write something about the victorious loser. They know that I came out for Goldwater, and voted for him, and they have correctly guessed that I took a lot of abuse from the ever-tolerant, anticonformist liberals. Now, say the faithful, is my chance to get back at the people who said Goldwater was trigger-happy, that he would be sending more troops to Vietnam, that he would use atomic weapons, and so on; and that anyone who supported Goldwater was mad, mad, mad. Inasmuch as Johnson is doing the very things that he said Goldwater would do if elected President, why not gloat a little?

Friends, I gloat a little twice every day: in the morning when I read the newspapers, and at night when I tune in on the news programs. If I have not gloated in print it is only because I try to keep these messages lively through variety. As good a writer as Westbrook Pegler was, he finally became a bore by repetition. If you saw the name Eleanor in a column of Pegler's, it was a column you could skip, and the first duty of a journalist is to stay readable. As a former sports writer (and none better), Pegler should have known how to mix them. The temptation to become a pamphleteer need not be irresistible to a journalist who does not shut out other interests. Some of the best writing Pegler or any other journalist ever did was in his final months as a columnist, in those reminiscences of his early days in the newspaper business. They unfortunately came too late. Pegler had driven his people away, and William Randolph Hearst Jr. was being shielded from the Pegler talent by Bob Considine and Frank Conniff. Considine, who could be called the greatest living reporter if I could be called Harvey Cushing, is—to put it delicately—inhospitable to superior talents. It would surprise me very much to hear that he threatened to resign if Hearst fired Pegler. As for Conniff, the newspaper shop-talk is that he ghosts the pieces that appear under Hearst's byline, and, like Gore Vidal, he ran for Congress. He inherited, if that is quite the word, Pegler's position on the comment page of the New York *Journal-American*. But even without the assistance of Considine and Conniff the non-revolving door had opened outward for Pegler, and he had principally himself to blame.

So I learned a little lesson there. However, as I have not said much about Goldwater in the past four or five months, he has not become a tiresome topic of these messages. I am inclined to believe that as a presidential nominee he is through. But as a man with a following he has to be reckoned with. From letters and conversations I surmise that his following is virtually intact, and until a stronger man comes along Goldwater will continue to retain his leadership. He still has the largest following on the Republican side.

In the East we hear of quiet activity on the part of Richard Nixon. It will get nowhere. Nixon made a political mistake in moving to New York. Although he lost the California governorship to Pat Brown, he might have won next time out. By changing his residence he dissipated his local strength, and in New York he certainly will get no help from Nelson Rockefeller or Jacob Javits. In spite of the left-handed assistance he is getting from the misbehavior of the Democratic legislature, Rockefeller can be counted out, and he would not support Nixon anyhow. Javits is not a Republican Republican, and in any other state but New York he would not get Republican support. Nixon's political future is that of a young elder statesman. The fantastic thought comes to me that if he were to run for anything in New York, Jim Farley could beat him.

It is deplorable that so much of the nation's news is processed through New York City, where the men and women who do the processing are largely of the liberalistic stripe. (Washington is no better, only smaller.) The liberals on the newspapers, the magazines, television and radio are emotionally incapable of presenting the conservative viewpoint without prejudice. Consequently the nation as a whole cannot become acquainted with the possible successors to Goldwater. The only young man you ever hear of through New York is John Lindsay, the forty-five-year-old congressman who is always mentioned with Javits and the New Jersey senator, Clifford Case. Lindsay is acceptable to the liberals, and well he might be.

In the past ten years on every major campus there has been the sound of the young conservative voice, in spite of the noisy liberals' efforts to drown it out. It is Goldwater's duty to help make that voice heard. Gloating is not voting.

May 22, 1965

Abandoning all caution, I now hazard the guess that history will judge that Winston Churchill did more to win the Second World War than Edward R. Murrow. This may seem like a rash, reckless statement when the newspapers and the air-waves—very particularly the airwaves—are so full of posthumous salutes to Murrow. Nevertheless I take the risk. Thirty years, or one generation, hence, I may have to eat these words, and that will be an unpalatable repast for a man of ninety.

The only time I ever met Murrow was at a party at the home of Miriam Hopkins. The New York home of Miriam Hopkins, I should say. It was a charming small house on the East River, which Miss Hopkins still owns. There, and in Beverly Hills, her parties were unique, or at least atypical of the parties usually given by movie stars. Most of her guests were chosen from the world of the intellect: novelists, playwrights, musicians, composers, painters, sculptors, directors, government officials. They were there because Miriam knew them all, had read their works, had listened to their music, had bought their paintings. They were not there because a secretary had given her a list of highbrows. At that party, which was about twenty-five years ago, were Edward R. Murrow, Vincent Sheean, John Gunther, and William L. Shirer, among many others. Sheean, who likes to bait people, had been baiting me for not having fought beside Hemingway in the Spanish Civil War. It was a pretty good example of what would now be called putting me on. Before I could reply, Murrow said quietly, "And what were you doing there, Jimmy?"

I never knew why, but Murrow's question crushed Sheean, and I didn't have to say a word. Murrow winked at me and grinned, and I smiled my thanks. It was the only time I ever actually met Murrow, but of course I remained kindly disposed toward him.

But after the war, when he returned to New York, CBS did a varnish job on him and he was not an unwilling object of the glamorizing treatment. He was a radio announcer who had been converted into a war correspondent, and with his elocutionary gift he was equipped by nature and by temperament for a whole new career. In an earlier day he would have made a splendid Chautauqua artist; in the late 1940s he was transformed into a quasi-official voice of the liberal movement. And though I was voting that way myself, and usually was in agreement with the words Murrow uttered, I considered him a ham.

The more popular he became, the hammier he got. The elocutionary style was being developed—the dramatic pauses seemed to be controlled by a stop-watch, the voice was pitched a half-tone lower. And of course the bolder he got in the scripts he read, the higher his rating as a statesman-without-portfolio.

He was much better off than if he had had official status. As a public official he would not have enjoyed the immunity that he was granted at CBS, where only William S. Paley could fire him. Another bit of luck in his favor was the fact that he had not pursued his theatrical career. At Washington State College he had been a member of the National Collegiate Players, a recognition society in dramatics. After college he abandoned the stage, and by not becoming a professional actor he escaped the attainder that was slapped on every actor, right or left, who spoke out on political matters. Murrow closed the curtain on his interest in amateur theatricals. He mentions the National Collegiate Players in his 1946-47 Who's Who sketch, but not in the succeeding volume.

It is also interesting to note that in the 1946-47 sketch he cites his membership in Scabbard and Blade, which is a national collegiate military society. Its purpose, according to Baird's Manual, is "to raise the standard of military training in American colleges and universities, to unite in closer relationship their military establishments, . . . to promote preparedness for proper defense of the United States by disseminating accurate information . . . concerning the military needs of the nation." After 1947 Murrow ceased to proclaim membership in Scabbard and Blade, although he continued to acknowledge Kappa Sigma; and he apparently picked up an honorary membership in Phi Beta Kappa along the way. I wonder if Phi Bete knew he had been in Scabbard and Blade.

I rapped him several times while he was still in good health, and ten years ago I declined the supreme honor of one of those Person-to-Person interviews of his. I had, and have, nothing much against him except that he was overrated and never questioned the overrating.

May 29, 1965

No one can seriously question Thornton Wilder's eligibility to any high literary award, foreign or domestic. He began with an original turn of mind, which he trained and disciplined, and the durability of his work has already been demonstrated in his lifetime. His twenty-seven-year-old *Our Town* is probably the great American play. His first novel, *The Cabala*, published in 1926, which I reread last winter, is a work of art. Almost forty years ago Thornton Wilder, with that book, established himself as a major figure on the literary scene. And in 1965 the most popular song of our time, "Hello, Dolly," comes from a musical comedy based on a Thornton Wilder play. On the personal side, he is and for many years has been one of my favorite people, a dear man and wonderful company.

But if there can be no demurrer to Thornton Wilder's qualifications for high honors, there can be and are some doubts as to the eminence of Mrs. Lyndon B. Johnson as a literary critic. Naturally anything she says about anything stands a good chance of being quoted, and when she is encouraging the residents of Washington, D.C., to cultivate window-boxes, she is on firm ground. Until very recently, however, her opinions on literary matters have not been much in demand. It now appears that she has been positively bursting with literary comments that needed only the right moment for public expression.

The moment arrived when a committee voted to give Thornton Wilder another gold medal and $5,000. Through connections that are fairly obvious to me but that I will not go into here, the committee arranged to have Lady Bird make the presentation in the White House. Here was the opportunity she had been waiting for.

I do not know how Mrs. Johnson works: on the typewriter, or with pencil or ball-point pen. It is possible that she gets assistance in having her manuscripts retyped, and she may even accept a little professional help in putting her ideas into shape. One or two sentences in her presentation speech led me to believe that she was open to suggestion from outside sources. I'm afraid, though, that she must accept full responsibility for a rather tactless performance. Accidental tactlessness is one of the marks of the amateur.

As she gave Mr. Wilder his nice presents she said, among other things: "Unlike some modern writers, you respect your fellow man and you respect the American language. You have never confused being modern in language with a dreary reliance on four-letter words. You have never assumed that realism in writing means a cloying self-pity or a snappish disdain for others. You have written with an understanding, affectionate rapport with your subjects which to me is the hallmark of genuine literature."

Now what is that but the kind of literary comment that you might expect from a Goldwaterite? Last summer, only last summer, Lady Bird's husband was getting vigorous support from the very authors whose names come to mind as you read her speech. Yet she was compelled by political expediency to hold in her true feelings about American literature and the practitioners thereof. John Dos Passos and I stood practically alone on Goldwater's side, while all those authors whom Mrs. Johnson secretly despised presented a united front for LBJ.

Nor was her tactlessness merely political. Although I do not recall that Thornton Wilder has ever been attacked on grounds of obscenity, I doubt that he was made more comfortable by Mrs. Johnson's insistence that he typifies Nice-Nellyism. Also, while I did not see a guest list for the presentation ceremonies, I assume that among those present was the Johnsons' great friend, John Steinbeck, whose books have been barred as many times and in the same states as mine, and for the same reasons. Steinbeck must have squirmed a little. It must be difficult to know what to do in a case like that, when the wife of the President of the United States is saying so positively things that you cannot possibly agree with. The only time I ever met a wife of a President of the United States, she said many things I could not agree with, and my wife and I excused ourselves and made our exit. But that was at a party in a private house. In the White House I guess you just sit there and take it. You're not supposed to leave before He or She does.

Lady Bird would be well advised to stick to her window-boxes. But I wouldn't count on it. She told the Wilder audience that the talent she most envied was "the ability to make words march and sing and cannonade and talk the cool, demanding voice of reason." Too bad Meredith Willson writes his own lyrics.

June 5, 1965

Back again, we are, to the somewhat mysterious desire of the present federal government to take away the individual citizen's firearms. Let us commence with the remarks of Senator Thomas Dodd (D-Conn.), who said, "A powerful lobby is spending millions" to defeat a bill to restrict the sale of firearms.

A powerful lobby, says the senator. Well, that makes us think of sinister and jolly fellows who try to corrupt our legislators with fur coats, electric iceboxes, junkets to golf tournaments, loose women, and actual cash. That's the picture we retain of "powerful lobbies spending millions." It so happens, though, that laws exist which were written to restrict the activities of lobbyists and to protect our legislators from temptation. If Senator Dodd has knowledge that these laws are being violated, it is his duty to denounce the lobbyists and to see that they are prosecuted. In his own state of Connecticut the senator has constituents who are employed by the Colt Patent Fire Arms Manufacturing Co. of Hartford, and they have the power to deal more effectively with the senator than I have.

On the subject of lobbying, however, it should be noted in passing that the senator has the support of the most powerful lobby in Washington. I refer to the executive branch of the present federal government. They seem to be going all-out on this bill. Although you might think that the attorney general of the United States had other things to do to keep him busy, he got into the act. If you did not see Nicholas deB. Katzenbach testifying, and only read his testimony in the papers, you missed a performance. The printed word did not do justice to the Justice Department. "As long as I live," said Katzenbach, "I can never forget that it was a mail-order rifle, sent to a post-office box, that had been rented under an assumed name, by a man with an established record of defection and mental instability—that killed President Kennedy." The trouble with using that sort of emotional appeal is that if it is not completely convincing, it just lies there. It can be made convincing by a Walter Huston or a Gary Cooper, professional actors; or it can be convincing when the emotion is genuine and without regard for its propaganda value in putting across a bill. Mr. Katzenbach is not Walter Huston or Gary Cooper. He is, on the other hand, a cabinet officer who was on The Hill to do something the administration wants done. It should be pointed out to Katzenbach and for all others who use Kennedy's assassination for their own purposes that at Runnymede, throughout the dedication ceremonies, Mrs. John F. Kennedy conducted herself with great dignity and restraint and made the ceremonies memorable by so doing. It has been impossible for me to visit the Lincoln Memorial in Washington without feeling a strong emotion, but when I have been there I have not had Katzenbach or anyone else to spoil it for me.

The day after Katzenbach did his share, Senator Robert Kennedy (D-N.Y., ex-Mass.) and a man named Thomas C.

Lynch, the California attorney general, had their say. The proceedings, by the way, are being conducted before the Senate juvenile delinquency subcommittee. I mention that fact because Bobby Kennedy and Lynch talked about secret organizations such as the Ku Klux Klan, the Black Muslims, the Minutemen, and the ease with which they obtain machine guns, mortars, and anti-tank guns. (On exhibition in the committee room was an anti-tank gun that had been purchased by three youths for ninety dollars. An anti-tank gun is not something you slip into your vest pocket, although you could get it into your station wagon.) A subcommittee on juvenile delinquency, in other words, becomes the forum for a discussion of delinquency that is quite senior. But that makes little difference to our legislators, who have a way of tacking on riders to bills that bear no relation to the riders. Domestic disarmament has the backing of the administration, and the subject might just as easily pop up in a hearing of the powerful Committee on Waste Papers, the powerful Armed Forces Committee, or the powerful Ways and Means Committee.

In this naughty world we all have a tendency to look out for No. 1—ourselves. Our selfish interests creep in. For instance, the night before the Katzenbach testimony, my mailbox was vandalized. Several weeks earlier my summer cottage and those of four neighbors were broken into and burglarized. The police cannot be everywhere. But I freely confess that if I had surprised the vandals on either occasion I'd have used my burp gun, if I had one. I know of several law-abiding citizens who feel the same way.

There has been some pressure on me—not enough to crush a grape—to say something about the state of prizefighting. All right.

In a court of law an expert is required to state his qualifications, or the opposing counsel concedes them. Since there are some readers who concede me nothing, I shall state my qualifications on this subject, and graciously concede that they are dubious.

From age five to age ten I took boxing lessons from my father's chauffeur, a Negro named Arthur Woodward. Whatever I learned I usually forgot in the heat of battle. In my early journalistic career I covered prizefighting on about as low a level as you could get. Mickey Walker once came to my home town, counted the house, and refused to go on. In later years I attended many fights, in the course of which I became an admirer of Joe Louis, Henry Armstrong, and not many others. In a sense the high point of my attendance at the fights was when I escorted Tallulah Bankhead to the Louis-Baer fight. In another sense, the high point was the first Louis-Schmeling fight, when I won $1,000 from a movie director and $500 from a drama critic, neither of whom has paid me to this day. The only friend I ever had in the fight mob was the late Hymie Caplin, who died shortly after he got out of prison where he had been doing a bit on a crooked-gambling rap. I have known lots of others, but Hymie was the only one I would call a friend of mine. The last fighter I met was Rocky Marciano, to whom I was introduced by Humphrey Bogart. I liked Marciano, and still do, but as Bogart died in 1957 it is obvious that I have not been keeping in close touch with boxing.

The simple truth is that I don't give a damn about prizefighting and haven't for a long time. I would not pay ten dollars for a ringside seat for a world's heavyweight championship fight if they held it in Trenton. Trenton is less than ten miles from my house. I might watch the fight on TV, but if Peggy Lee were on the Johnny Carson show at the same time, I doubt if I'd look at the fight. Why?

Well, apart from the fact that I have no more interest in present-day fighters than I have in present-day tennis players, the excitement of a business that was always a business vanished when I became finally convinced that the business was a racket. Through the years I saw many fights in which the losers appeared to be doing half-gainers, but I used to believe that most of the important fights were on the level. Now I have a hard time believing that any fight is on the level.

The prizefight racket has reached the point where professional wrestling has been since the days of Jimmy Londos—and it might be safer to say since the days of Frank Gotch. An entire generation has grown up without ever taking wrestling seriously. It exists only as a TV performance that has its appeal among the devotees of Soupy Sales, young and old. That is what prizefighting has become, and from now on it should be so regarded.

The populace grew restive and remained so for all of thirty-six hours after the Clay-Liston exhibition. With the help of some alert politicians, there was a noisy demand for federal investigation of the prizefight racket. But that doesn't really make much sense. It is conceivably within the jurisdiction of the federal government to provide the kind of protection that is aimed for under the Pure Food and Drug Act. It is a duty of the federal government to provide for the common defense. But federal supervision of the prizefighting racket is another matter. I do not believe that the federal government should abolish prizefighting. In principle, at least, I do not even believe that the federal and state and local governments should use their taxation powers to put prizefighting out of business. If the chumps want wrestling and prizefights, let them have it, and let them have it as long as they want it. When they come to the right stage of weariness and cynicism, they will stop going to the fights and cease to watch them on TV. Until then prizefighting will be profitable, and money talks, and it talks the same language to the racketeers and the TV executives.

An honest fight is, of course, a disgusting and degrading exhibition on the part of the participants and the onlookers. In an honest fight one man is trying to kill another man, and sometimes he succeeds. Pugilism is less revolting than a contest in which the two men have at each other with meat cleavers, but the basic idea is the same. A fixed fight is a mean thing because the chumps who watch are deprived of their money's worth of manslaughter.

June 19, 1965

Although I have been needling Mr. and Mrs. Lyndon B Johnson (and will continue to do so as I see fit), when the invited me to their residence at 1600 Pennsylvania Avenue Washington, D.C., I accepted their invitation. I was bette brought up than the poet Robert Lowell, who apparently wa not taught that when the President of the United State invites you to the White House, you damn well go. Lowel was invited to a Festival of the Arts at the White House accepted the invitation, and then decided that since he wa opposed to the Johnson policy toward Vietnam and th Dominican Republic, he would withdraw his acceptance. Sai Lowell: "Every serious artist knows that he cannot enjo public celebration without making subtle public commi ments." To that I say, "Rats!" And for the private benefit of my Beacon Street readers I might even say, "Wharf Rats!"

I was not invited to the same function that Lowell so pompously decided not to attend. My invitation was for a party in honor of the winners of the presidential scholarships, at which Mr. Johnson gave the students their medals, and after which there was dinner followed by an entertainment program. Obviously I was invited for one reason and one reason only: I am a member of the National Institute of Arts and Letters (of which Lowell is also a member). When I was introduced to the President we shook hands; I said, "How do you do, Mr. President," and he, I fancied, rather grumpily muttered something. Mrs. Johnson was gracious and said, "A pleasure to know you, Mr. O'Hara," every syllable articulated. As I was wearing a plastic badge with my name on it in large letters, I am unable to say whether Mrs. Johnson identified my classic features or the lettering. However, I am able to say that no commitment, subtle or otherwise, was given or sought.

All through the party I kept looking about to see how many other serious artists had braved the hazard of a public commitment. Marianne Craig Moore and John Updike were there. Paddy Chayevsky and Louis Auchincloss. Karl Shapiro and S. J. Perelman. Stan Musial and Dr. Jonas Salk. Colonel John Glenn and Tom Lea. The Brothers Four and Jason Robards Jr., as well as various press and radio-television individuals of varying degrees of artistry and seriousness, who were not there on assignment. How much soul-searching went on among these men and women after Lowell's impudent refusal to add his personal prestige to the White House it is impossible to guess, but they were there.

Poets are strange people, and Lowell poets are not the least strange. Robert Lowell's kinswoman, Amy Lowell, used to embarrass her brother Larry, then president of Harvard, with her habit of smoking cigars in public. Her public commitment to Havana leaf was at a time when ladies had not yet won their battle to smoke cigarettes out in the open. It was also at a time when A. Lawrence Lowell, as president of Harvard, was carefully campaigning to acquire cash from the Harknesses and other tycoons. But it is one thing to blow cigar smoke in the face of your brother, who happens to be president of Harvard, and it is quite another matter to give the bird to the President of the United States. When he invites you to the White House, you damn well go.

On my visit to Washington I was reminded by my surroundings of an anecdote about Henry L. Stimson, a man whom I always greatly admired. One day President Theodore Roosevelt was driving through Rock Creek Park in the company of Elihu Root, and in the distance they saw a young man on horseback. Root recognized the young man and mentioned to Roosevelt that he was an able and promising lawyer named Stimson. Roosevelt waved to Stimson, signaling him to join him. Immediately, unhesitatingly, Stimson plunged his horse and himself into Rock Creek and rode the straightest line to the President's carriage. Soaked to the skin, he saluted T.R., and said, "At your service, Mr. President." Then and thereafter Henry Stimson was at the service of the United States of America.

In the language of people like Robert Lowell the action of Stimson would be called chauvinistic. It is one of their favorite words, and indeed was used by Lowell in his windy explanation of his nonappearance at that Festival of the Arts. The word is oftener misused than not, and you would expect a poet to be more precise than Lowell was when he said that "we are in danger of imperceptibly becoming an explosive and suddenly chauvinistic nation." But poets are strange people, and a rose is a rose is a rose. Or is it?

June 26, 1965

During a lifetime that has not been notable for its Spartan simplicity I have paid a great many visits to Washington, D.C., and spent a great deal of time in Hollywood. Inevitably I wrote a piece some years ago in which I pointed out the similarities of the two places. They were one-industry towns, I said, and I even got around to the similarities of the respective press corps: Arthur Krock reminded me of Louella Parsons, Joseph Alsop of Hedda Hopper. If I were to bring the piece up to date I suppose I would argue that James Reston occupies a position similar to that of Sheilah Graham. Walter Lippmann has no opposite number in Hollywood, as he has remained aloof from the mouse-race in Washington; but surely David Brinkley has achieved the status of a Jimmy Fidler.

The trouble with such analogies is that once you have made the point of the fundamental similarity between the one one-industry town and the other, it becomes a game in which you force resemblances of things and people where no real resemblance exists. Washington is not an institution that submits to continual light treatment any more than Hollywood should be taken as seriously as the producers would like it to be. And yet the vulgarity of the Washington social life would be startling and depressing if it were reported with the same seriousness as the capers of the Hollywood characters.

The excuse for the Washington social life has always been that the statesmen must be able to relax. But in a large measure the social life and the relaxation have become an end in themselves. In the thirty years that I have been visiting Washington, I have seen an increase in the size and number of parties at which the statesmen were outnumbered by the out-of-towners. That, to be sure, is one way for a statesman to relax, especially if he is a readily identifiable ham. But there is a vast difference between the relaxing small dinner party and the big blasts that New York and Atlanta and Los Angeles and Detroit citizens flock to by the hundreds. Am I against such parties? Certainly I am. They vulgarize the purpose of the capital city with the same disrespect as the exhibitionists who chain themselves to the White House fence.

Somewhat less spectacular are the men and women who have private income, who secure a more or less tenuous connection with the federal government (or none at all), and settle in Georgetown because it's fun. Fun it is, and no doubt about that. It is more fun to put on your new Givenchy for the party at the French Embassy than it would be to doll up for a dance with the same old crowd at a Long Island or Los Angeles country club. They are silly, useless people, but they are not altogether harmless. They have money, they often have acceptable social credentials, and they have some skill in the minor art of wriggling through the transition from one administration to the next. But they represent a concentration of gossip and rumor-mongering that deals with the individuals who are running the country and not just the country club, and as such they are a nuisance or worse.

Ideally, Washington as a one-industry town would conduct its business along the lines of a Gary, Ind., or a Provo, Utah. The business of government is government, as Calvin Coolidge never said, and there is already so much of that that the sidelines should be carried on elsewhere. The culture-vultures who wish to have an Athens of America but are dissatisfied with Boston are referred to Athens, Ohio, which already has a fairly old university. The party-lovers are urged to try Newport, R.I., which now offers a jazz festival, and New York, N.Y., which is not only a party town but is also almost as unsafe at night as the District of Columbia itself. During the Eisenhower administrations and since the coming of Lyndon B. Johnson, culture and chic fared less well than they might have. During the Roosevelt administrations culture began to creep in with the arrival of all those intellectuals, and culture became chic under Kennedy. This may be the moment for a dispersal of the elements that only confuse the statesmen and distract them from their duties. But I am not too optimistic. The White House has "cultural advisers" who are not going to give up easily, and the notion that cultural activities might be transferred to Athens, Ohio, is of course fantastic. Cultural activists are gregarious and like to watch each other swoon.

As for those big bashes, it will take more than the Martin Market to put a stop to them. Just as long as a hundred-dollar ticket to a ball is tax deductible, our senators will be offered that kind of relaxation, although George Murphy is probably the only one who could do the frug.

July 3, 1965

Forty-one years ago this month I entered the newspaper business, and I have been in and out of it but never far away from it ever since. I love it as much as I despise some of the men in it. Among the legitimate enterprises only the game of politics contains more men who are afflicted with venality, envy, and gutlessness; and not even in holy orders will you find men who are touched with a greater zeal for truth and honesty and decency. The moment I enter a newspaper office I am at home, not only because the surroundings are as familiar to me as backstage is to an actor, but because, like the actor, I am ready to go on in any part. I could write a headline, take a story over the telephone, cover a fire, or interview a movie queen, and if I had to make up the front page I could do that too, although I might not win the N.W. Ayer Award for it. In Dublin a few years ago my wife went to see the Book of Kells, and I spent the afternoon in one of the local newspaper plants on a tour of inspection. The same thing might occur in any city in the world. Incidentally I never did get to see the Book of Kells.

With such devotion to this business I am dismayed whenever there is a rumor that any newspaper is about to fold. The rumor that the New York *Herald Tribune, Journal American,* and *World-Telegram* were talking merger implied, of course, that two metropolitan newspapers were folding. This was amended to a later report that the papers were discussing an arrangement whereby they would all three use the same printing plant, etc. The curious thing about the early rumor was that it has been circulating for at least three years, but suddenly was treated as a news story by NBC and *The New York Times.* To suggest that NBC and the *Times* were impatient to see the rumor come true would be to reveal my own suspicious nature, but they certainly hammered away at a rumor that was not spot news. Nor was any time lost in their reporting that the labor unions were alerting U.S. Attorney General Nicholas Katzenbach to the possibility of antitrust-law violations in a merger of the three papers.

Having revealed my suspicious nature, I might as well confess that if I were the owner of a competing newspaper, I would see some advantages in having my opposition go broke or become so unprofitable that it would be foolish to continue publication. In such circumstances I would also see some disadvantages if my opposition were permitted to consummate a merger. A successful merger might offer stronger competition than I had had to meet in the past, and if I could get the attorney general to use the resources of the federal government to fight the merger, I would be very grateful.

The newspaper situation in New York City is said to be precarious. The *Herald Tribune* is owned by John Hay Whitney, who is not likely to go broke, and who has other enterprises so profitable that they can carry his newspaper. The *Journal American* is published by William Randolph Hearst Jr., and the *World-Telegram* is a Scripps-Howard affiliate. I do not pretend to have the inside dope on the

Hearst and Howard finances, but it is probably reasonable to guess that Whitney needs their help less than they need his. That leaves the *Daily News,* a money-maker; the *Post,* a sheet that I do not find indispensable, but that may have some usefulness to the big labor unions; and the *Times,* a large-sized newspaper published on West 43rd Street. The *Daily News* and the *Times* appear to be the only profitable English-language papers in the nation's metropolis, and if worse comes to worst, they may turn out to be the only ones to survive.

The nearest thing we have to a national newspaper is the *Wall Street Journal,* which is well written, well edited, widely circulated, and highly profitable. But it is not yet what people call a regular newspaper, the kind they are accustomed to; it is adjunctive to other newspapers, not read for itself alone. This leads me to my big idea for this week.

An organization called the Free Society Association, of which Barry Goldwater is honorary chairman, is causing some consternation among Republican National Committee members because it threatens to raise funds among Goldwater supporters. The money is to be used for a "crusade of political education." My suggestion is that the FSA take over one of the New York papers and spend the money for a national newspaper. With a circulation list of 27,000,000 men and women who voted for Goldwater, plus a few million disillusioned individuals who thought they were voting against his policies, such a paper might actually end up in the black. It is inconceivable that it would end up in the red.

Men are getting ready to land on the moon; the four-minute mile is now a commonplace; I have been on the wagon for twelve years; all sorts of things that once were considered improbable are today accomplished facts. What man has not done, man may just possibly do. I still don't give William F. Buckley Jr. much chance of getting elected mayor of New York City, but if the water shortage should get so bad that the citizens desert the city by the millions, leaving only a few hundred stalwart Buckley supporters to vote, he might win.

Buckley himself, of course, does not expect to win. No Conservative candidate is ever likely to be elected mayor of New York. If Bobby Kennedy, Jacob Javits and John Lindsay should get together and decide to raid the Conservative movement as they have raided the Republican and Democratic organizations, they might be able to put up a candidate—George Jessel, say, or Dwight Macdonald—and win on the Conservative ticket. At present, however, it is Buckley who is running.

The ungrateful New York newspapers ought to thank him for running. He is the only man among the announced candidates who shows any promise of providing readable copy. *The New York Times*, in an editorial, stamped its foot with a petulance that revealed a deep fear that Buckley might take a few thousand votes away from Lindsay. The *Herald Tribune* conceded Buckley's right to run, but insisted that "the principal business before the city of New York this year is electing a mayor, not staging esoteric debates." John Hay Whitney, publisher of the *Herald Tribune*, has not been

110

in the newspaper business very long, and may be forgiven for not having learned that under the American system political debates, esoteric or slapstick, are almost meaningless if they are not carried on during election years. Apparently the *Times* and the *Herald Tribune* agree that Buckley has the right of free speech in off-years, but should not say anything that might lure votes away from their candidate. Lindsay is going to win anyway, now that Robert F. Wagner has withdrawn from the contest, but it is characteristic of liberals and liberal newspapers that they admire dissenters only when they are dissenting on their side. Holmes and Brandeis were acceptable dissenters, but you never heard a word from the liberals about the dissenting opinions of Mr. Justice Pierce Butler.

Buckley's decision to campaign gives promise of some interesting months ahead. He has announced that he is not going to kiss babies or eat pizzas, and I am sure he is not going to kiss pizzas or eat babies. Nevertheless he will provide newsworthy items. Whether the newspapers and the radio-TV people will give him coverage is another matter. Buckley has brains, and the TV mike-holders who are nervous in his presence show it by making little faces at him. The most disgraceful example of that discourtesy was given a couple of years ago when Jack Paar, who intellectually is not strong enough to carry Buckley's books, smirked and grimaced while Buckley was a guest on Paar's own program. The same thing occurred on the same network the night Buckley announced his candidacy. Buckley has an agile mind, an impressive fund of information, and a forensic manner that drives his inferiors in all departments into confused fury.

Now that Bobby Kennedy has set a modern precedent, it would be much more interesting if Buckley, who has plenty of dough, would carpetbag election to the U. S. Senate in some safe state. Buckley may have some such thought in mind. I've never met him, and come to think of it, I owe him a letter in reply to a friendly note he sent me a while back. Whatever his intentions may be after this campaign, he really belongs in the Senate. Perhaps Oregon could be persuaded to elect him as a replacement for Wayne Morse. I can think of fifty other senators for Buckley to replace, but

Morse is such a chronic dissenter that Oregon might accept Buckley in his stead. Buckley, unlike Morse, has never been kicked in the head by a horse; but he is a yachtsman, and he could point out to the Oregon electorate that a fellow can get an awfully mean crack from a swinging boom. Yes, Oregon might like Buckley.

Realistically, the price on Buckley's getting elected to any important office should be about 100-1 against. Buckley can afford the bundle of money and the four months of his time that his mayoralty campaign will cost him; but it would be unfortunate if he were to waste the time and the money on this campaign alone. He must campaign as hard as if he had a chance of winning, right down to November 2. He has undertaken the responsibility of presenting the Conservative case in the most anti-Conservative city in the nation.

July 17, 1965

The late Bernard Baruch was an attractive gentleman who had enough dignity and charm to withstand the devotion of certain of his admirers. As is so often the case when a distinguished man dies, the race to proclaim friendship with him in print ended in a tie between the right ones and the wrong ones. The Broadway characters, possibly with the advantage of a crouching start, ran a dead heat with the more substantial citizens. And yet the feeling persists that Baruch in death was every bit as effective in maintaining his position as he had been in life. There is no record that commits him to a mutuality of confidence with those individuals who for years had been making the curious claim that they always went to him for advice. He did not go to them for advice; they went to him. And on this evidence they boast of an intimacy that I never found convincing. In New York there is an advertising slogan, "You have a friend at Chase Manhattan," that invites us to borrow money from that particular bank, but as far as I'm concerned the Chases who are friends of mine are a family in Waterbury, Conn. I would never expect to be asked to play poker with the Manhattan Chases, but with the Waterbury ones I have. By the same token, the men who sought his advice seemed to be stretching a point.

Baruch's position vis-à-vis his non-intimate friends reminded me of one of the banking Rothschilds of Paris, who owned a racing stable. An acquaintance tried to borrow some money from Baron Rothschild, and the baron regarded him as a poor risk. "However, I shall be at Auteuil for the races tomorrow," said the baron. "You may come and stand in my box." Such public association was as good as money in the bank for the would-be borrower, and it didn't cost Rothschild anything.

By the time I met Bernard Baruch he was already an elderly man, older than I am now, and he had the protection of that famous hearing device which he would turn off and on when he didn't care to listen. Consequently he did not catch my name (a difficult one for deaf people anyway) the only time we ever had dinner together, although I found later that he had read some of my books, and spoke well of them. Thereafter he made a point of being polite, but I was never able to verify a remark he is said to have made on the question of betting on the horses. As a modest horse-player myself, I regard the remark as a classic. It was repeated to me by the late Bill Corum. "No man ever committed suicide," Mr. Baruch is said to have said, "who had a horse in the winter book." A so much more picturesque way of saying that hope springs eternal.

One of the reasons that it is difficult to accept the Broadway sharpies' intimacy with Baruch at their own valuation is that he was the same Bernard Baruch who could refer to a President of the United States as a "rude little man." Of course Harry S Truman might be rude to Bernard Baruch where some of the advice-seekers would not dare to be, but it is hard to believe that a man as independent as Baruch would be so patient with his hero-worshipers. In an earlier message I spoke of Winston Churchill as being a public man. Baruch was a public man, one of that special breed who achieve a thirty-fourth degree of their own freemasonry. They are not like you and me, and it is foolish to expect them to be. In more ways than one they turn off their hearing aids; they have special glands that secrete a glazing-over substance for their eyes; they have special manners that they adopt that are as natural to them as sleepwalking to somnambulists. It takes fifty years to develop the public man and the public manner, although the signs of both begin to appear much earlier. Oddly enough, the manner is not acquired by practice, and never by actors. A few actors possess the combination of charm and dignity that is basic to the public man, but the genuine manner emanates from the habit of power, the power of wealth or authority or both. Somewhere in the background of power there is even the power of life and death, to stay an execution, or to break a man financially, or to have him machine-gunned in a South Side garage, or to ruin his reputation. Baruch mixed with power all his life, and predictably he was a public man at an early age.

Power is not an abstract thing, even when it is not in use. It is therefore a continually fascinating subject, through Lord Acton to Lion Feuchtwanger to this casual study of Bernard Baruch. We whose power is limited sometimes console ourselves with the observation that it is self-destructive and corrupting. But isn't it remarkable how many old men hold on to it to the very end?

July 24, 1965

My reasons for switching from lifelong, straight-ticket Democrat to independent conservative are too abundant to deal with in a short piece. But one reason for continuing as an independent conservative is that it is more fun.

The stereotype of the American conservative is not as well defined as David Low's British Colonel Blimp, which is a classic. In this country we have Peter Arno's Union Club type, the huff-puff gentleman with the busty wife who wears her mother's pearl choker. The Arno caricature is perfect as far as it goes, but it has a limited circulation, confined to the readership of *The New Yorker* magazine, while David Low's Blimp became known to the masses. Perhaps if Arno had given his character a name it would have caught on, and the American conservative would be represented by something better than Grundy.

It is probably too late to suggest a name for Arno's man, but C. A. Peters, or Curtis A. Peters, might be acceptable, if not particularly catchy. (It happens to be Arno's real name.) In any event, Arno's huff-puff and Low's Blimp, good though they are, misrepresent the conservative to the extent that they imply that we have no fun. We do have fun, some of us.

Now I am sixty years old, full of aches and pains and infirmities that reduce my vigor and deny me my whisky. I am probably a grouch. But I get my laughs at the expense of the liberals and the intellectuals. As an independent conservative I belong to the Outs, and yet I need not conform to the policies and restrictions of the Outs if I don't feel like it. When I was a New Dealer I had to conform or be banished.

The New Dealers screamed about orthodox religion, censorship, nazism, fascism, capitalism, and so on, but they submitted to a degree of thought control that would have irked a Trappist monk in a monastery. Indeed, a staunch New Dealer friend of mine escaped from his companions by becoming a Trappist, a rather desperate measure that seems to have suited him but would not appeal to me.

Although, as John Hersey once said, I take the tragic view of life, it is impossible to ignore the comedy. For instance, Johnson and Dirksen. The man who nominated Barry Goldwater has become, in less than a year, Lyndon Johnson's most dependable supporter in the Senate. For instance, Johnson and Adlai Stevenson. The liberals very nearly smoked out Stevenson a week or so ago; they not only got him to admit that he was not always in agreement with the policies of the administration, they very nearly picketed him right out of the United Nations. The liberals remember (and so do I) that Stevenson was a dove during the Bay of Pigs conferences, and was in disagreement with the stand that John F. Kennedy took. Stevenson is an ambassador, not a policy-maker, and as an ambassador is inhibited by precedent, but it is kind of fun to imagine what he and Johnson really think of each other.

For instance, Johnson and Bobby Kennedy. The press is now so full of their feud that I need not dwell on the details of it. But there must be sleepless nights in the White House when the President wishes he could replace Bobby with a genial, tractable man like Charles de Gaulle. My only meeting with Bobby was a brief one a year ago at the Bohemian Grove encampment, when I had an opportunity to observe him close to. He gave a set speech (which he repeated elsewhere, so let's not have too many complaints about Ronald Reagan and his set speech); and then he mingled with friend and foe, and I met him the next day at a breakfast party. I thought then, as I do now, that there is something pathetic about a man who turns on the charm when he has none. In the long run, as history adds up the score, Bobby Kennedy may turn out to be just that: a pathetic figure. He is, shall we say, overcompetitive. As a wheeler-and-dealer he is overcompeting with a wheeler-and-dealer who learned the name of the game under Sam Rayburn and Alben Barkley.

The most fun, of course, is in being a conservative and a professional journalist (as a paid-up member of Sigma Delta Chi, I am entitled to call myself a professional journalist). The sympathies of most journalists are with the liberal Democrats, and the writers of the think pieces often have to look the other way when an awkward situation arises between Johnson and Stevenson, Johnson and Bobby Kennedy, Johnson and Mansfield, Johnson and the Big Unions and the professors and the civil righters and any of the other groups or individuals that he tries so hard to please. The pro-conservative journalist need not look the other way, unless it hurts him to laugh.

July 31, 1965

I am in the midst of preparations for a trip to England, Scotland and Ireland. This trip was planned before Mr. Johnson asked us to do our touring at home, and is not in defiance of his wishes. Like many of my fellow-citizens, I am not in much of a mood to defy Mr. Johnson right now; he has it tough enough. Also, I am so heartily in favor of his appointment of Henry Cabot Lodge as ambassador to Vietnam that a spirit of bipartisanship has me momentarily in a loose grip. Let us hope that Lodge's appointment has not come too late. Let us devoutly hope. The failure of John F. Kennedy to make Lodge Secretary of State in the first place cannot be rectified, but Kennedy's failures were not confined to his cabinet selections. They just happened to be more conspicuous than some others.

Mr. Rusk, an uninspired workhorse, seems to be headed for pasture-land, for no spectacularly dramatic reason, and it does not take a soothsayer's talent to guess that Lodge will succeed him. It will be a rather cruel correction of Kennedy's odd rejection of the obvious qualified man. Kennedy, after all, did appoint Douglas Dillon and Robert McNamara, who were Republicans, but the logical man was Lodge. How long Lodge would have lasted in a Kennedy cabinet is conjectural, and yet interesting because the conjecture is instantaneous, automatic. Kennedy and Lodge had opposed each other in a political campaign, with Kennedy emerging victorious, and there were such fundamental differences between the two men that they might have been unable to work together. It would not be the first time that the President of the United States and his Secretary of State failed to see eyeball to eyeball. Nevertheless I somehow have faith in the Johnson-Lodge coalition, if only because their fundamental differences are so much more different from those that existed between Lodge and Kennedy.

These observations, strangely enough, are part of the preparations for my trip to Britain and Ireland. I have bought my "steamship" tickets, for wife, self and automobile, and booked hotel reservations for wife, daughter and self. The word has gone out to my friends, and my business associates are sharpening their wits. In view of the fact that I shall be at the wheel of the car on our journeys, the islands' populace should be alerted. My car is English, but with a left-hand drive, and those foreigners are just going to have to be extra careful. If I can go to so much trouble to make my visit a pleasant and mutually profitable one, those people ought to do their share.

Most of the people I will see are politically Liberal or Labour. Not all, but most of them. They are considerably more polite about my switch to the conservative side than American liberals tend to be. The last time I was in London I helped to celebrate the Conservatives' victory, and it's possible I may bring them luck again. They were worried about Nixon. Not that he would lose, but that he would win. I had lunch at White's Club, which is not a hangout of the radical left, and my companions were made uneasy by my prediction that Nixon would make a good showing if he did not actually win. Despite their conservatism and their lingering hostility toward Joseph P. Kennedy from his ambassadorial days, they had somehow convinced themselves that Jack Kennedy would be more sympathetic to Britain's problems than Nixon.

The Liberals and the Labour people were, of course, terrified that Nixon would get in. The foolish notion that the British take their politics lightly is as absurd as the legend that their favorite comestible is Brussels sprouts. You can get Brussels sprouts if you ask for them, but if you ask for them you deserve them. The myth of lethargy during a British political campaign is strictly American journalese, as unreliable as the fictional contrast between an orderly British football crowd and the rowdyism of a game between the Detroit Lions and the Cleveland Browns. In Liverpool and Glasgow people get killed over football arguments. (They get killed here, too, on the day of the Yale-Harvard game—in motor accidents on the way home.) And while I was not threatened with bodily harm by my Liberal and Labour friends, they implied that I had gone crackers because I wanted to get home in time to vote for Nixon. Goodness knows what they would have implied if they had heard me say I was voting for Goldwater.

What I try to do in England is to correct some of the false impressions and misstatements that are sent back to the British press by their New York and Washington correspondents. The men and women who represent the foreign press in this country are generally so hidebound liberalistic that they see no other side. They are wasting their papers' money by being here at all. They share their employers' hostility toward the U.S., a circulation ploy that pays off in Britain. The idea is a continuation of lend-lease; Bertie McCormick originated it in Chicagoland, with his one-man war against Britain.

August 7, 1965

Noel Coward once said that some women should be struck regularly, like gongs. But since my approach to women is not fundamentally the same as Noel Coward's, I have hesitated to make the gong technique a canon of my procedures and attitudes. Although I may often have felt like belting a woman, I have never actually taken a poke at one except in anger. That, of course, is not the same thing as the Coward method, which clearly states that they should be struck "regularly" and says nothing about provocation.

Actually, a man never wins in a public quarrel with a woman, no matter what the provocation or the degree of violence entailed. Our civilization is so constructed that a guy just doesn't look good in a hassle with a dame. It can be a dispute over alimony, or it can be a controversy between a cardinal and Mrs. Roosevelt. In every case, if your sympathies are with the man, you still wish he had stayed out of the thing. Regardless of the result, he comes out covered with feathers, if not tar. Therefore I am grateful to Richard Burton for sticking his two cents into my small wrangle with Elizabeth Taylor.

A few years ago Miss Taylor was under contract to M-G-M and owed that studio one more picture. She was getting $150,000 a picture. Along came 20th Century-Fox with an offer of $2,000,000 for her to appear in their film, *Cleopatra*. Metro, however, insisted on her fulfilling her contract with them, and they cast her in a film based on my novel, *Butterfield 8*. The then Mrs. Eddie Fisher let out a yell that could be appraised at $1,850,000, or the difference between

her Metro salary and the Fox offer. That part was understand-
able; I like money, too. But Mrs. Fisher issued a statement
in which she gave the remarkable opinion that the heroine of
my novel was "practically a prostitute." Bear in mind that
the part she was eager to play was Cleopatra, not Joan of
Arc. Bear in mind, too, the fact that Mrs. Fisher had already
been Mrs. Todd, Mrs. Hilton and Mrs. Wilding, though not
yet thirty years old, and had long since changed her public
image from that of the little girl who loved a horse in
National Velvet.

The corporate villain was Metro, which insisted on her
making *Butterfield 8* according to the terms of the contract.
The film won for Miss Taylor the Academy Award. I have
yet to see it, but I have seen a lot of newspaper and
magazine clippings of her disparaging my novel. History tells
us that Miss Taylor went on to give a performance of
Cleopatra that got mixed notices. I haven't seen that, either,
but presumably she was comfortable in the role.

The cracks she took at my novel gave me some small
bruises which were healed by the Metro accounting department with tender, loving royalty checks. No one would say I
was grateful to Miss Taylor, but I was inclined to let bygones
be bygones, until her present husband belatedly got into the
act. (Miss Taylor had got her then current husband, Fisher,
into the act by insisting on having Metro give him a part in
Butterfield 8, and I hear he was terrible.) But now Miss
Taylor and Richard Burton are on display in something
called *The Sandpiper*, and Burton, in publicizing this dog,
took occasion to comment that my novel was a "piece of
rubbish." It really wasn't a piece of rubbish. I had nothing to
do with the writing of the film, but the novel, published in
1935, was ahead of its time and is treated a lot more
respectfully today than most novels published three decades
ago. Mr. Burton, who is a hell of a good actor, had better not
make any predictions on the durability of *The Sandpiper*,
which he went into with his eyes open and, inferentially, did
not regard as rubbish. The most complimentary, if not the
only complimentary, comment I have seen about *The Sandpiper* is that it is reminiscent of *Rain*, the 1922 play by John
Colton and Clemence Randolph which was based on a short
story by W. Somerset Maugham.

Mr. and Mrs. Burton, who in private life are Richard Burton and Elizabeth Taylor, seemed to have elected to appear together in a piece of rubbish. They seem to have done so in a wearily contemptuous manner that so irritated the movie critics that they have been warning the public of what to expect. The notices read more like warnings than reviews, and "Ars Gratia Artis" may have to be changed to "Caveat Emptor." Or even "Cave Canem."

This is not the Burtons' first offense of this kind. They entered the tripe market a few years ago with a thing about goings-on at the London Airport. I saw it on a voyage on the *Queen Mary,* and I was glad I was not traveling by the BOAC. I don't anyway, if I can help it, but the Burtons almost made me airsick. Open the porthole, Richard.

August 14, 1965

With care and caution I have been reading the journalistic requiems over Adlai Stevenson, which contained no surprises by the liberals but did present some remarkably unpredictable reactions by the reactionaries. William F. Buckley, for instance, wrote not one but two pieces about Stevenson that were so full of admiration that they could just as easily have been written by someone on *The New Yorker.* As a matter of fact and opinion, Buckley's eulogies were more graceful than *The New Yorker*'s anonymous article.

By a morbid coincidence I happened also to be plowing through the Arthur Schlesinger Jr. pieces in *Life* about John F. Kennedy, and I discovered that Schlesinger did not like

Kennedy. He worked with him, he has written a book about him, he compliments him, but he did not like him. He of course does not say so, but inescapably comes the conclusion that in the opinion of Arthur Schlesinger Jr., the late President was somehow undeserving and ill-qualified. The inevitable inference is that Kennedy was not quite astute enough to realize that in Schlesinger he could have had another Harry Hopkins. My guess is that Kennedy may have been astute enough to realize that if he didn't watch out, in Schlesinger he might easily have had another Harry Hopkins.

I don't think Harry Hopkins liked anyone, and Schlesinger cannot hide his own patronizing attitude toward Kennedy, which was so similar to Hopkins' expedient devotion to Roosevelt. Not to be elaborately euphemistic about it, I always considered Hopkins a bit of a jerk. (The feeling was mutual.)

Here and there, among the pretty things that liberals had to say about Stevenson, would crop up little indications that the liberals had some reservations about him. So many references were made to his wit and eloquence that it was like a biography of Chauncey Depew or a prepared obit of George Jessel. The writers then would snap out of it and remind themselves that they were not eulogizing an entertainer but a symbol of the liberalistic movement. Then would follow an excerpt from a UN speech, or a paragraph from one of his speeches made during one of his campaigns. A couple of sticks of type, as we say in this business. But that would be followed by some biographical material that liberals do not customarily play up in pieces about their heroes. The aristocratic background. The club memberships. The pleasure he took (and was looking forward to) in the country gentleman atmosphere of his farm in Libertyville, Ill., surrounded by Republicans.

The relentless snobbism of the liberals is nothing new, of course, and they like to feel that some Groton and Porcellian and Social Register rubs off on them. Gilt, as someone must have said, by association. But liberals also like to feel that such people as Roosevelt and Stevenson and Mrs. Peabody and Mrs. Tree have totally deserted the old life and are forming the nucleus of a society of chic progressives. Only up to a point will the liberals tolerate the continuance of old habits among their idols. When FDR took himself out of the Racquet and Tennis Club, and John Hay Whitney took himself out of the Social Register, the liberals were delighted. But *The New York Times* in recent years has been giving a big play to the Racquet Club-Social Register kind of life, which is indicative of the liberals' ambivalent longing to be part of an existence that officially they must deplore. (One of the most conformist liberals I ever knew once confessed to me that his secret ambition was to become a member of the Paris Jockey Club, and he didn't know a fetlock from a crupper.)

The first time I met Adlai Stevenson was at a party in my house after a Yale-Princeton game. He was insufferably pompous and ill-mannered. The second time I met him was last spring, and he couldn't have been more charming. Seven years had passed between the two meetings. At the second meeting he sat next to my wife at dinner and told her, as apparently he was telling many people, that he was having a hard time making up his mind what to do with the rest of his life. He wanted to get out of public life, but he was not sure he wanted to return to Libertyville and the private practice of law. His death occurred before he could announce his decision, if he had made one. But it is going to be interesting to see what the liberal biographers make of his indecision. In view of what Schlesinger has already done to Kennedy, it will be interesting to see which of Stevenson's admirers (while he was alive) leads the posthumous attack on him.

August 21, 1965

I have been reading the galley proofs of my forthcoming novel while at the same time, if not the same minute, involved in the writing of a novel that will not be published before 1967. The reading of galley proofs is a thankless chore, a period of drudgery between the satisfaction of completing the writing of the book and the always new pleasure of holding the actual bound volume in your hand for the first time. I have published more than two dozen books, and I still get a charge out of opening the parcel that contains the latest one. As has been noted a thousand times before, it is the nearest a man comes to the proud, protective emotion a woman must get when they let her hold her baby for the first time. It is the unavoidable cliché, but I never discussed it with my mother, who had eight children, or with Mrs. Joseph P. Kennedy or with Mrs. Frank Fontaine.

This time, however, the advent of a creative effort of mine is clouded over by a destructive threat that I had nothing to do with. My book is to be published (officially) on Thanksgiving Day, and by that time we may once again be in an all-out war. I don't think we will be, but by the logic of events we should be. One thing, as they say, leads to another, which is what I mean by the logic of events. It will take a powerful piece of illogicality to disturb the present sequence, and the disturbance may be no more than a postponement.

And yet I (and you) must go on planning for 1967. You must go on planning to add a new room to the house, a new child to the family, and all the other changes and improvements that you contemplate in spite of the destructive threat.

If you and I defer to the destructive threat, we only expedite it. We participate in it. We cannot pretend the threat does not exist; we will be getting daily reminders of the reality of it.

Three decades ago the Nazis and the Communists were trying out new weapons and techniques in Spain—and I was just getting started on my book-writing career. Like all good liberals at that time, I gave my sympathies to the side that opposed our eventual enemies, the Nazis. Our ultimate and current enemy, the Communists, seemed by far the lesser of the two evils, and not until four years later, when they signed the nonaggression pact with Adolf Hitler, were we able to see ourselves for the innocent, simple-minded chumps that we were. Shortly thereafter the Nazis made chumps of the Communists, and we were back again on the side of the U.S.S.R. Now this bit of history—some of which is conveniently forgotten by diehard liberals—has had no effect on the individuals who stayed in the liberal movement. But it can also be confusing to those of us who left it. Good Americans are being killed in a war that is even more remote from us than the civil war in Spain. Now, in 1965, we are in somewhat the same position as the Nazi supporters of Francisco Franco thirty years ago. Opposed to whom? Opposed to Communists. They are trying out new weapons and techniques in Vietnam, and so are we. (It isn't Chinese guided missiles that knock down our airplanes.)

The temptation is strong to come out for isolationism, especially when Dean Acheson has recently come out strongly against it. But to become isolationists now we would have to break the habits of fifty years, beginning with the help given the Allies in the First World War, through the Second World War and on down to our enormous but casual commitments in Southeast Asia. Notwithstanding the fact that we have become Uncle Ugly to the world, we have conditioned ourselves to a compulsive giveaway addiction. That being the case—possibly in incurable one—you and I must somehow on our level, go on planning as we have done. You make and sell what you have to sell, I make and sell what I have to sell, and the federal government will collect the taxes to support our national addiction. Acheson, who may be one of the world's greatest authorities on stupidity, declares that isolationism is stupid. Well, yes, in a way. If isolationism is going to require that we cold-turkey ourselves to cure our addiction, it would be stupid not to try to find an easier method.

I suggest that the easier method is for you and me to risk the Acheson invective by indulging in a form of isolationism that he might not catch onto. While working hard, as I said before, we give the appearance of being too busy to take any position on international affairs, regardless of the daily reminders of crisis. We may then find that we are, as they love to say in Washington, de facto isolationists. They could accuse us of passive resistance, but Gandhi made that fashionable. He died by violence, but we all gotta go sometime.

August 28, 1965

Once in a while we who report the mood of the people would do well to remember that there is no such thing as the mood of the people. There are many moods of many people, and the best we can ever do is to observe and report on a single mood (or trend, or attitude) at a time. We can guess, but only guess, at the proportion of the people sharing that mood.

Summer is a disruptive time, with the citizens and their families off on vacations, but it can make our job somewhat easier. Because they are on vacation and not at home, in the past few days people from Kentucky, California, South Carolina, Florida, and several Middle Atlantic States have been telling me what they are thinking. As it happens, they are mostly WASPs—White, Anglo-Saxon, Protestants—but not many of them voted for Goldwater, and most of them were saddened by the death of Adlai Stevenson. It is a piece of liberalistic silliness to assume that WASPs are as rigidly conformist as the liberals themselves. The WASPs are not even all conservatives, but among those who are you will find as many shades of opinion as there are WASPs, because the conservative movement is the gathering-place for individuals. Rugged or not, individualism flourishes in the conservative movement. How sweet it is!

Nevertheless there is, I believe, a unanimity of confusion among conservatives that is shared by the liberals and by Dr. Gallup's old reliable Undecideds. There seem to be at least three sides to every question, more or less hotly contested by the various partisans. The major question is, of course, the problem of Vietnam. We the people sit with our hands folded, if not manacled, while Mr. McNamara leads us on to war. Criticism of McNamara has an implication of approval of the policies of our many enemies, domestic and foreign, that is almost unavoidable. The last thing I want is war, but the next to last thing I want is to offer the slightest support to anti-Americans at home or abroad. What do you do in a case like that? Suspend criticism of McNamara? Hope that Henry Cabot Lodge will produce a miracle?

The character of the man who is now President of the U.S. is, I think, responsible for the confusion that afflicts us. During last year's campaign I referred to him as a man whom no one loves and no one hates. He has seen to that, and during the campaign he qualified as one of Dr. Gallup's Undecideds. But once elected he should have performed a miracle on himself and abandoned the habits of a political lifetime. The U.S. cannot afford a President who performs like a politicking senator part of the time, and the rest of the time dreams of greatness. There is a large amount of greatness of a sort inherent in the office itself. You are sure of your place, of a place, in history. Events that require the presidential attention are bound to identify him with the bigness of the events. But Johnson is not content with that. This ill-equipped man has convinced himself that he is as tall in the saddle as Abraham Lincoln and Franklin D. Roosevelt. But does anyone else believe that?

There are moments when Senator Dirksen appears to be doing the thinking for the country. There are other times when we appear to be guided by Senator Mansfield. And now and then we get scraps of information that could be taken to indicate that we are governed by a Washington law firm. The truth, no doubt, is that Dirksen, Mansfield, and the law firm are influential and useful, influential while they are useful. The absurd pretentiousness of the Great Society, which is government by slogan, occupies our leader's attention until he is compelled to make some utterance on the situation in Vietnam. But he stays with that no longer than he has to, because he is more at home at home. Because he has not changed his ways, because he remains the politicking senator, he knows how to divert our attention with spectacularly political appointments and vote-catching enterprises.

It is not the shadow of John F. Kennedy that bothers Mr. Johnson. He can always exorcise that wraith by dedicating another monument or, in a different mood, by taking a whack at Bobby Kennedy. (I wholeheartedly grant him the latter pleasure.) My guess, which will never be anything but a guess, is that Mr. Johnson often thinks of Harry S Truman, who was no ball of fire either. But when Mr. Truman gave the order that exploded a ball of fire over Japan, something happened to him. Nothing like that will happen to Lyndon Johnson. That was Goldwater who was going to use that step to greatness.

September 4, 1965

At a recent gathering of writers an author asked me if I had been given many honorary degrees. Inasmuch as I rather suspected that he already knew the answer, I told him the truth. No honorary degrees. He pretended to be astonished, so I laid it on pretty thick, and in so doing I departed from the factual record. No college or university had ever offered me an honorary degree, I said. That was a fib.

College A offered me a degree several years ago. The offer was accompanied by a thorough and complicated outline of a scheme whereby I would turn over all of the rights to my next novel. That meant that College A would receive all royalties, including the paperback and motion-picture monies. With the money College A would build a library, name it after me, and give me an honorary Litt. D. It was a breath-taking proposition, not only because it was so brazen, but because the economics professor appeared to know as much about my financial affairs as the Internal Revenue boys. Indeed, he knew more. The Internal Revenue agents who are assigned to authors seem to have been chosen for their total lack of experience or information in my line of endeavor. In any event, I told College A that I would think it over. I am still thinking it over, seven or eight years later.

University B also offered me a degree. Two members of the faculty called on me one day to invite me to become a member of the university English department. As I had already contributed numerous manuscripts and other items to their library collection, I was inclined to think I had done enough for a university with which I had no real connection, family or otherwise. So I thought I had a good out when I said I had never gone to college, and lacked the academic qualifications for the associate professorship they wished me to take. "Oh, we'll take care of that," said one of my visitors. "We'll give you an honorary something or other."

My third opportunity to tack some letters to my name was with College C. I had heard very little about College C. Indeed, I had it mixed up with another college with a somewhat similar name in the same geographical neighborhood. This is unusual for me; through the years I have acquired a vast amount of information about colleges and universities. Not only the obvious oddities such as the fact that Cornell and Columbia are in Iowa as well as in New York; but I know that if you are a student at Rio Grande you are about two thousand miles from the Mexican border, and if you are a student at Dropsie College you are not studying medicine. I am a walking Baird's Manual. But I did not readily identify College C and I was so touched by their wish to honor a total stranger that I said I would appear at their commencement.

I arranged for the charter of a small airplane to get me there and back. Unfortunately the flying weather that day was unfavorable, so I had to cancel the flight and my appearance at the ceremonies. Then I learned that College C wanted me in person; no show, no degree in absentia. That night I watched "What's My Line" on the television and was pleased to find that College C had given an honorary degree to Arlene Francis. As Miss Francis is an old friend of mine, she would have been pleased to accept my parchment and deliver it to me, but apparently that was not suggested.

In a long and (I believe) useful literary career I have received five major honors. Not to be bashful about it, they are: the National Book Award; membership in the National Institute of Arts and Letters; the Gold Medal of the Academy of Arts and Letters; the Critics Circle Award and the Donaldson Award. You will note that among them is no recognition by the institutions of higher learning, a fact which tells as much about them as it does about me. Why? Because no week passes during which I fail to receive some invitation on the college level, either to conduct a seminar, to officiate as a writer-in-residence, to judge a literary contest, to contribute to the literary magazine, or to give a lecture. It is baffling. If they would agree on a unanimous policy of disapproval of me and my works, as they agree on a policy of nonrecognition, I would be less confused. But the letters of invitation to perform the chores they want me to perform are written in highly complimentary terms—much more complimentary than the language of degree citations. I get about two hundred such letters a year. The five major distinctions, however, were awarded me by other writers, not by the professors, nor by the professors in conjunction with college trustees.

Friends say, "You've done all right, why care about honorary degrees?" Well, there is a practical side to it. If Yale had given me a degree, I could have joined the Yale Club, where the food is pretty good, the library ample and restful, the location convenient, and I could go there when I felt like it without sponging off friends. They also have a nice-looking necktie.

September 11, 1965

I like to think that at Tuskegee or Fordham or the University of Washington there is a young Negro who is quietly watching what is going on, and does not like what he sees. I like to think that this mythical young man, who would be someone on the order of Bill Cosby and Bob Teague, is taking a cold and dim view of the activities of Martin Luther King and James Farmer and Dick Gregory and Cassius Clay and James Baldwin, and of the white men who are so free with the epithet Uncle Tom and its verb form Tomming.

This deeply disturbed young man is in for a lot of unhappiness. The vituperation he will get from the Baldwins and the Kings will be so discouraging that he may want to give up—in which case he is not my man. My man will not give up. He will not give up under attack by his own people, or succumb to the blandishments or the insults of white politicians. He will have to learn to be suspicious of white-colored or black-colored people who yap about the brotherhood of man. Is there a brotherhood of man, and if so, just what does it mean? And when did it begin? I do not wish to be a brother to Bishop James Pike or to Surkarno or to Frank Sinatra or to Louis Auchincloss, and I will not have a true fraternal feeling for Sammy Davis Jr. or Bobby Kennedy, even at the point of a gun. There are people I like and people I don't like. Thirty years ago there was a Negro entertained called George Dewey Washington, who always finished his act with the statement, "I want you to know that your applause goes to my heart and not to my head." The statement used to go to my stomach and turn it. The late Richard Wright once told me that a story of mine was the only one about Negroes by a white author that he could take. But I did not then become a brotherhood-of-man salesman; I reserved the right to go on thinking that Pearl Bailey is just as much of a bore as Sophie Tucker, and that Ella Fitzgerald is as fine an artist as Gladys Swarthout.

My mythical student will find out soon enough that the brotherhood of man is a term that is usually invoked when someone is making a pitch; whether it's a religious or political or charitable pitch, the pitchman wants something, whether he's wearing a Roman collar or a Brooks Brothers shirt. Having learned that great truth, my man is ready for some others. He will learn, for instance, that it will surely take five hundred years (and maybe five thousand) before cross-breeding of the races produces a tan that will be the uniform color of all human skin. The human toe may disappear before all our descendants are of the same color. (The human race itself, of course, may disappear the day after tomorrow, but we are leaving out that possibility as too frivolous for this serious discussion.) But when this toeless tan man, with his plastic organs and transistor brain, has been perfected, the creature will still find something to quarrel over. That is basic to the human condition. I am not a reader of science fiction. I am sixty years old, and the crazy stuff I used to read in *Popular Mechanics* when I was a kid is all commonplace now, and I can't go through that again. But while the soul of man remains, the need to do something naughty will linger on. My mythical student will know these things because he will be smarter than I was at his age. Knowing them, and being smarter, he will decide for himself how far into the future he wishes to lead his race.

For that is what he will be—the leader of his race. He will not be the leader of my race, any more than Abraham Lincoln was the leader of the Negro race. He will not waste his time in declamations of his pride in being a Negro or in the conventional eulogies of George Washington Carver and Booker T. Washington. He will have to deal with my people, because we have the money. But he will be smart enough to know that when he deals with politicians, the federal government politicians and the ward heelers, he must be careful not to sell his vote. The vote is being sold now, today, in the process of being bought by civil rights and antipoverty programs that are so inextricably identified with the Democratic Party that the Republican Party is being eliminated. My mythical student will be taking a particularly hard look at the development because he is smart enough to know that when the Republican Party has been nullified, the Negro will have only one place to go. And the vote that he has fought for will be useless in a one-party system.

I have striven to avoid making the hard-sell pitch in these messages, and it is an exercise in futility to make a pitch to a mythical man. But if my mythical man is real, I urge him to consider the hazards of the one-party system. It would be tragic if my mythical man remains a myth because the Democrats have a monopoly on the mythical brotherhood of man.

September 18, 1965

It is so easy to find Biblical comparisons to the age in which we live that we may have a tendency to ignore them as too obvious. For the moment, let's not ignore them. There are wars and rumors of wars; weird things are happening in the skies; we have floods in the West and drought in the East; Connecticut and New Jersey have reported plagues of serpents; brother is turning against brother; fire and pestilence have broken out; men worship strange gods or none at all; sins of the flesh are a commonplace.

If I sound like a road-company Billy Graham there is a reason for it: I listen to Billy Graham on the radio, and have done so for many years. I also listen to Charles E. Fuller and his honey; and to other evangelists and preachers, Greek and Reformed and Lutheran and so on. This is a side of me known but to a few, including Henry R. Luce. For a brief period I was—and this always gets an incredulous laugh—religion editor of *Time* magazine. In my tweedy, not to say checkered, career I have hustled a buck in some odd ways. If as a religion editor I resembled Elmer Gantry more closely than I did John Roach Straton, who is to cast the first stone? Well, they were cast, and I was cast out like devils by Beelzebub. It was as close as I ever came to the occupancy of a pulpit, but religion has always fascinated me. More accurately, morals have always fascinated me, albeit somewhat less intensely than sin.

The temptation, therefore, is to start with the Biblical comparisons to our times and write a jeremiad that would correspond to a 20th-Century version of the Old Testament.

It could be done. The material is here, Big Sin is everywhere, and for the first time in history we know for sure that mankind can be destroyed, not by a wrathful Jehovah but by man himself. The end of the world is at hand if we push the right buttons, and that's a fact. But the prospect of obliteration is so big that most of us are incapable of understanding it. A sort of unrealistic optimism keeps us from a comprehension of the danger that we accept as factual but reject as unimaginable. We don't really get the big picture, because we don't want to get it.

Very well, let's have a look at a picture that we *can* understand. We are living in the Age of the Jerk. The manifestations of Jerkism are all over the place and limited to no class or race. It is Jerkism when Negro hoodlums loot a shoe store; it is Jerkism when a manufacturer refuses to lower his prices after the excise tax has been removed from his product. It is Jerkism when Ivy League types commit vandalism at a debutante party, and Jerkism when Bronx teenagers drop down to the Yankee Stadium outfield to steal Mickey Mantle's cap. It is Jerkism to boo Mantle and Pepitone when they come to bat. It is Jerkism to carry a roll of toilet paper to the Yale Bowl, and Jerkism to participate in an outlaw strike. It is Jerkism to lie down on the floor of the White House or on the tracks of the Southern Pacific to "protest" anything. It is Jerkism to keep a ten-foot boa constrictor in a college dormitory, and Jerkism to mislabel a food product. It is Jerkism to drink three Martinis, and Jerkism to pretend that Pop Art is Art. It is Jerkism to pretend that a newsphoto is a picture of Jackie Kennedy when it obviously is not Jackie Kennedy. It is Jerkism for a boy to grow his hair like a girl's, and Jerkism for his mother to think it's cute. It is Jerkism for a nonrabbinical student to grow a beard, and Jerkism for a John Bircher to accuse Eisenhower of communism. It is Jerkism to be a Communist, and Jerkism to be a John Bircher.

The list is a dreary recital and endless, with additions available every time you read your newspaper or take a train ride or witness TV. Some of the items are no worse than tick bites, some of them are symptomatic of afflictions more serious, but all of them in varying degree are warning signs of weakness. It is not enough to say that standards are changing. That excuse implies that when the changes have occurred, new and better standards will take their place. I see no reason to think so. The total rejection of the standards and principles that we know were good will make it extremely unlikely that honesty and decency will be revived. Honesty and decency and the other virtues were not native to the Stone Age man. It took thousands of years to achieve them, many more years than they have been allowed to exist. They never achieved universality, and now it looks as if they never will. The great irony resides in the fact that in the fight against disease and injustice and cruelty we have come to the Age of the Jerk before we came to the universality of decency, and in the fact that the Jerk is often the most vociferous opponent of injustice.

September 25, 1965

The nuns were great on geography. My very first schooling was at Miss Katie Carpenter's, a small and exclusive institution where I learned to read and write at an unusually early age. The logical next step was Mrs. Thurlow's, which took you through grammar school, after which you went on to Mercersburg or Andover or Westover or Shipley. But my local Ivy League education was abruptly terminated by my mother's belief that my sister and I knew more Protestant hymns than Catholic, and she was right. We were on the way to becoming High Church Episcopalians, and my mother was a Sacred Heart girl. So off we went to St. Patrick's and the Sisters of St. Joseph, where we became closely acquainted

with the Studs Lonigans of our place and time, and I got a
cassock and surplice and raised my mother's foolish hopes
that she had produced a Jesuit.

No experience is wasted on a writer, therefore I may have
profited by the extracurricular associations with my schoolmates. Some of them were miserably poor, walked eight
miles a day, carried lunches that consisted of large hunks of
bread and slices of rat cheese, and were hosts to insects in
their scalps. I remember all that and more of the same. But
the book learning I got from the nuns was mostly orthogra-
phy, etymology, syntax, prosody—and geography.

There were forty-eight states then, and before I was ten
years old I could recite all the states, their capitals, and the
bodies of water on which they were situated (Dover, Dela-
ware, on Jones Creek; Tallahassee, Florida, inland; Mont-
pelier, Vermont, on the Winooski; Columbia, South Carolina, on the Congaree). Next came the boundaries. "Master
O'Hara, bound Connecticut."

"Connecticut. Connecticut is bounded on the north by
Massachusetts, on the east by Rhode Island, on the south by
Long Island Sound, and on the west by New York."

"That is correct. Now bound Wyoming."

"Wyoming? Wyoming. Wyoming is bounded by uh . . ."

We were taught the Principal Products, and some effort
was made to get us to memorize the year each state was
admitted to the Union. A total loss. But many years later I
pleased and astonished Robert Benchley by my ability to
name the counties of Massachusetts. I had not learned them
from the nuns, but from them I had learned to look at maps
with something better than the dull hostility that I felt
toward the multiplication tables. (And I had been in every
county in Massachusetts.)

The nuns did not confine themselves to the U.S. Oh, by no
means did they. We plodded all the way down from Baffin
Land to Tierra del Fuego, taking in all the countries and
their capitals, their volcanoes and rivers and mountain
ranges, and the names of the missionaries who had first
visited them. Then we nipped over to the Eastern Hemi-
sphere and gave it the same treatment. When I was ten years
old I could draw you a line that pretty accurately matched

the course of the Yangtze-Kiang, and I did not have to stop and think of the name for Persia.

Now, when we need it more, geography apparently is not being taught as thoroughly as we were taught it in a parochial grammar school in Pennsylvania before World War I. The nuns themselves were not very well educated women. Most of them probably had the equivalent of a high school diploma and a two-year normal school certificate, if that. But they had been taught geography by other nuns, and I wonder why. The Ku Kluxers would have a ready answer: part of the Catholic conspiracy to rule the world from Vatican City. If that was the case, the program was a failure, as it was not coordinated with a campaign to hate anybody. Even Lucifer got some breaks. So it may have been that the Sisters of St. Joseph, a comparatively obscure order, made a specialty of geography and rudimentary cartography through the whim of some early mother superior. Whatever the reason, I am glad they did. I am appalled at the ignorance of geography that I have encountered among men and women who have graduated from prestigious schools and colleges. An intelligent woman of my acquaintance, who has been to Europe thirty times and speaks French, Italian, Spanish, and some German, confessed to me this summer that she always thought Iceland was somewhere up around Alaska. Too often I have caught overeducated men and women in similar bloopers.

I am not in the pay of Rand McNally, but it seems to me that a comparatively simple subject like geography offers a good start in a renaissance of learning in grammar school. Of course I am going on the assumption that the pupils have learned to read and write—a bit of wild optimism on my part.

October 2, 1965

My year is up, my contract has been completed and will not be renewed. This, then, will be the last of these messages.

For the reader who is curious, I vouchsafe this information. I was paid a lot of money to write these pieces, and most of it had to come from syndication. For a while it did, but even from the very beginning, from the first column, I got complaints from editors who seemed to have expected me to write a column that was like Walter Lippmann's for those who liked Lippmann, and like Art Buchwald's for Buchwald admirers. There were immediate cancellations by editors who had bought a column in which I could say what I pleased, but when it pleased me to say that I was going to smoke cigarettes, three editors announced that they were not going to renew their contract. I got them off the hook immediately. I told the syndicate to tell them to go to hell. So I lost those papers in the first couple of weeks.

It is an old story with me, this incompatibility with newspaper editors. They are a lot like movie producers. I once worked for a movie producer who was dissatisfied with a script I was writing. He made a remark that I shall always treasure as the most characteristic of the breed: He said, "If I don't get one of you writers to give me the script I want, I'll just have to write it myself." As if he could. He not only is no longer in the movie business; he bombed out of television. But he probably still thinks he could be a successful writer if he wanted to take the time—of which he now has plenty.

The newspaper business is full of men like that movie

producer, and I am not the first trained seal to tangle with
them. Writers as different from me, and from each other, as
Heywood Broun, Westbrook Pegler, Walter Winchell and
W. O. McGeehan, have had their troubles with desk men.
When syndication is involved, a bush-league editor (who may
be working for a big city paper) likes to king it on his
remote little throne. His paper may be paying something like
fifteen dollars a week for a column, but the editor can play
big shot by "firing" a writer he has never met, is not likely to
meet, and never should meet. The editor has convinced
himself that he, like my movie producer, could bang out as
good a column if he had the time.

Enough of that type did not like my column, and they
canceled. Those who stayed with it did not provide enough
income to keep the syndicate happy, and I was asked to take
a cut. That was something I would not do, so the syndicate
and I have parted company, and once again, for the tenth
time, I am an unemployed newspaper man.

I doubt if it will be for the last time. As long as I live I
probably will be getting jobs on newspapers and getting fired
or quitting. The virus hit me in 1924, has been with me ever
since, and certainly was not eradicated by this experience.
The pay was good, and the syndicate lived up to the letter of
the contract by sending out my columns exactly as I had
written them. I have no complaints there.

My experience does raise some doubt about the future of a
column that so unequivocally supports the conservative side.
My mail, from Boston to Seattle, contained the predictable
abuse by liberals and Democrats and beatniks. There was
some equally abusive mail from kook conservatives. But I
was touched by the sincerity and sometimes the anguish of
the men and women who feel helpless and lost in the country
they love. They got neither help nor guidance from me, but
they were like the people in a hospital corridor who are
waiting to hear about a relative's operation. They haven't
much hope, yet they must talk to somebody. For more than
thirty years I have been getting mail from strangers, personal
and intimate messages. But never have I read so many letters
of an unselfish nature—unless love of country is ultimately
selfish, as it may well be. The "You rat-fink!" letters have not
changed me at all, but there is no use pretending that I will

ever be the same after a really considerable amount of mail
that began, "Thank God for you." I can't go around the
country making speeches, because I am no good at making
speeches. Nor is journalism my work. Journalism is my fun,
and much of this past year has been fun. But now that the
year is over and I am retiring, I am beginning to wish I could
take that man in the corridor downstairs to the cafeteria and
buy him a cup of coffee. For no reason at all—since my
conscience is clear—I am beginning to feel like a rat. Not a
rat-fink. Just a rat. One of those creatures that abandon the
ship ahead of schedule.

My thanks and good wishes to you all.

Outstanding American Novels in SIGNET Editions

ELMER GANTRY   by Sinclair Lewis

One of Lewis' most scathing portrayals, the fiery novel of a golden-tongued evangelist who rises to power within his church, a saver of souls whose own life is one of hypocrisy, sensuality, and ruthless self-indulgence.

(#Q3090—95¢)

FLOOD   by Robert Penn Warren

Old crimes and forgotten indiscretions haunt the citizens of a Tennessee town on the brink of disaster.

(#Q2611—95¢)

THE GROUP   by Mary McCarthy

One of the most talked-about novels of recent years, this is the daring and brilliant story of eight Vassar graduates trying to cope with life and love during the turbulent depression years of the thirties. A United Artists movie release.

(#Q2501—95¢)

LIE DOWN IN DARKNESS   by William Styron

An outstanding novel about a tortured girl and the people and events that lead her to the brink of despair.

(#Q2655—95¢)

MARJORIE MORNINGSTAR   by Herman Wouk

A pretty New York girl sets out to become an actress, but finds her true destiny as a woman in love.

(#Q2156—95¢)

ATLAS SHRUGGED   by Ayn Rand

The great bestseller that tells the story of what happens to the world when the men of the mind—the men of ability —go on strike.

(#W3170—$1.50)

YOU CAN'T GO HOME AGAIN   by Thomas Wolfe

The turbulent years of the depression and the gathering storm clouds prior to World War II provide the background for Thomas Wolfe's brilliant last novel, the story of a sensitive writer trying to see life clearly and to convey the unvarnished truth.

(#Q3025—95¢)

GOD'S LITTLE ACRE   by Erskine Caldwell

Filled with passion, violence and humor, this moving and intimate story of earthy country folks has sold over eight million copies in the Signet edition alone . . . has been translated into 21 languages . . . and been published in 26 countries.

(#P3246—60¢)

Other SIGNET Books You Will Enjoy

THE HUMANIST IN THE BATHTUB by Mary McCarthy

Lively, controversial essays and criticism on the arts and contemporary mores, from the author's books, *Theater Chronicles* and *On the Contrary*. (#T2502—75¢)

SHADOW AND ACT by Ralph Ellison

The author of *Invisible Man* presents a series of essays on literature and folklore, Negro musical expression, and the complex relationship between the Negro American sub-culture and the North American culture as a whole.

(#Q3022—95¢)

UNDERSTANDING MEDIA by Marshall McLuhan

A provocative, widely debated theory about how television and other present-day mass media are changing the cultural patterns of American life. (#Q3039—95¢)

SOMERSET AND ALL THE MAUGHAMS

by Robin Maugham

The nephew of the late Somerset Maugham provides an enlightening family and personal history of the man behind the famous facade. (#Q3166—95¢)

BOGIE by Joe Hyams

The biography of Humphrey Bogart, a great star in his lifetime and now a cult hero for a whole generation who never saw his films while he was alive, written by a close friend of the star, with the authorization and cooperation of Bogart's widow. Introduction by Lauren Bacall. Thirty-two pages of photographs. (#T3071—75¢)

W. C. FIELDS: His Follies and Fortunes

by Robert Lewis Taylor

A Pulitzer Prize-winning author chronicles the life of one of our century's funniest men, a man whose private adventures were no less hilarious than his masterful performances. Illustrated with photographs.

(#Q3064—95¢)